Travel and Tourism

SAGE COURSE COMPANIONS

KNOWLEDGE AND SKILLS *for* SUCCESS

Travel and Tourism

Richard Sharpley

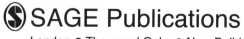

SAGE Publications

London ● Thousand Oaks ● New Delhi

First published 2006

SAGE Publications Ltd
1 Oliver's Yard
55 City Road
London EC1Y 1SP

SAGE Publications Inc.
2455 Teller Road
Thousand Oaks, California 91320

SAGE Publications India Pvt Ltd
B-42, Panchsheel Enclave
Post Box 4109
New Delhi 110 017

British Library Cataloguing in Publication data

A catalogue record for this book is available from
the British Library

ISBN-10 1-4129-2294-1   ISBN-13 978-1-4129-2294-4
ISBN-10 1-4129-2295-X   ISBN-13 978-1-4129-2295-1 (pbk)

Library of Congress Control Number: 2005935565

Typeset by C&M Digitals (P) Ltd., Chennai, India
Printed in Great Britain by The Cromwell Press, Trowbridge, Wiltshire
Printed on paper from sustainable resources

contents

This SAGE Course Companion has been written to help you succeed on your undergraduate travel and tourism course. In fact, it is rather like a travel guide! That is, it is designed to help you find your way around and make sense of the numerous and, perhaps, unfamiliar topics that are included in your course, pointing you towards key issues and concepts as well as directing you towards the most important books and readings. It will also help you undertake and successfully complete coursework assessments, and provide you with essential guidance to revising for exams. In other words, this Companion will help you on your journey towards achieving your degree in travel and tourism.

Of course, a travel guide is, by definition, simply a guide to a place you are visiting; its purpose is to help you make the most of your stay there but it cannot tell you everything you might wish or need to know. Similarly, this Companion is a guide to the study of travel and tourism, not a comprehensive course text. It is not intended to replace your lecture notes, textbooks and wider reading but, rather, to supplement them. Highlighting the important ideas, concepts and issues that you need to know, it will help you organise and structure your thoughts and learning, and it will enable you to make the most of your lecture notes, textbooks and other course materials.

As well as providing a focus for your reading, learning and research in travel and tourism, this book is also intended to guide you in your preparation of coursework and in your revision for exams, helping you to save time and avoid common pitfalls. In particular, it provides guidance and tips on what your examiners will be looking for in terms of key facts, concepts and arguments, enabling you to plan and write assessed coursework or prepare for your exams more effectively.

In addition to the subject specific information in Part Two of this book, you will also find a study, writing and revision skills guide in

Part Three. This is designed to help you learn more efficiently, to be a more effective student. Part of the learning process is attending and contributing to lectures and seminars but of equal, if not greater, importance is your use of textbooks and other course materials and your wider reading around the subject. This Companion will help you navigate this learning process, guiding your study of travel and tourism and helping you succeed on your course.

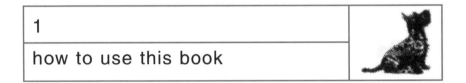

1	
how to use this book	

The overall aim of this book is to help you make the most of your travel and tourism course by establishing a framework for your learning about the subject and by providing essential help in completing coursework and revising for exams. Therefore, it essentially serves two purposes, namely, to support your learning and act as a revision guide.

To make best use of the book, then, you should use it to supplement your course textbooks and lecture notes by, first of all, making sure that you are familiar with the travel and tourism subject areas included in the book and where these are covered in your course syllabus. This means that you can then read about each topic before the relevant lecture or seminar, equipping yourself with knowledge of the important issues or themes and familiarising yourself with key thinkers or writers on the subject. Importantly, this will also help you to understand the relevance or contribution of any particular topic to the overall study of travel and tourism. As we shall see in a moment, one of the challenges of studying travel and tourism is that it is a broad subject that draws on a variety of academic disciplines. As a result, it is sometimes easy to lose sight of how particular topics fit into the overall travel and tourism picture.

Even if you do not wish to use the book to preview your course, you can use it both as a guide to preparing and writing assessed coursework and as an exam revision guide. It indicates the important elements of each topic covered, thereby helping to focus your reading and revision, and suggesting what issues and arguments should be included (or not included!) in assignments or exam answers.

Depending on how you want to use this Companion, therefore, you can dip in and out of it as your course progresses, you can prepare yourself by reading it in its entirety before starting your course, or you can just refer to it as a revision guide. Whatever use you make of it, however, you are strongly recommended to read the first section on studying travel and tourism. This looks at not only *why* we study travel and tourism but also *how* we should study it. In other words, at an academic level, travel and tourism is a diverse, fascinating subject that attracts interest from, or is explored within the context of, a variety of disciplines. For example, you will undoubtedly read books that look at travel and tourism from the perspective of business strategy, geography, economics, sociology, development or marketing, to name just a few. Conversely, at a practical level, travel and tourism is a vast and dynamic global industry and one in which many readers of this book may hope to work. It is important, therefore, that you can recognise the collective contribution of the different perspectives on travel and tourism to your knowledge and understanding of travel and tourism in the 'real world'. In fact, one of the key things that examiners look for is not only your knowledge of basic concepts and issues, but your ability to apply these to contemporary travel and tourism practice.

Part Two of the Companion looks at the travel and tourism curriculum in more detail, providing you with an overview of the key elements of each topic. Where these topics are taught on your course may vary as, currently, there is no standard travel and tourism curriculum. As a result, travel and tourism courses, in terms of the units or modules that are taught, differ considerably in their focus and design. Nevertheless, many, if not all, the topics introduced in this Companion will be covered at some stage in your course. Remember, though, that this section is not a substitute for your course textbooks – it is designed to give you a head start in learning about travel and tourism, and to provide a quick reference guide to coursework and exam revision.

Each topic covered within the section offers the following features:

- An overview of key concepts and issues, as well as hints and tips on understanding and using them. This will remind you of the main points to include in your coursework and exam answers.
- Running themes. Despite the diverse perspectives on the study of travel and tourism, a number of themes or issues run across the subject as a whole. Frequently, reference can and should be made to these in essays and exam questions.
- The contribution of key thinkers/writers on the subject. The ability to refer to or quote the work of key thinkers/writers in travel and tourism not only conveys a sense of 'authority' in your work but is also likely to impress examiners.

- Ideas for assignment questions. These should help you with the structure and content of typical coursework essay questions.
- Sample exam questions and sample answers. These should help you to anticipate and prepare for likely exam questions.
- Taking it Further sections. These introduce a more critical stance on contemporary and, perhaps, controversial questions or debates that are not normally covered in standard texts. Introducing these into your essays or exam questions is likely to have a positive impact on the quality of your work (and your grades!).
- A short list of key sources to focus your reading on the topic.

Students often have some difficulty in making the most of lectures and seminars, while they also need help with specific study skills, such as writing essays or revising for exams. Part Three of this Companion is a study guide which is designed to help you make the most of your lectures and seminars, and to develop your writing and revision skills. Finally, at the back of the book is a glossary of key terms that are used throughout the book and highlighted in **bold** at the first mention, as well as a comprehensive index.

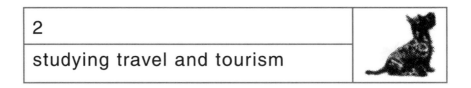

2

studying travel and tourism

Travel and tourism has been the subject of academic interest for well over fifty years. However, it was not until the 1970s, when a number of key academics began to develop a theoretical framework for its study, that it began to achieve more coherence as a recognised academic area. Its popularity as a course of study is even more recent. In fact, it is only ten to fifteen years ago that undergraduate programmes in travel and tourism became more widely available but, since then, the number of courses has, literally, exploded. So too, of course, has the number of students of travel and tourism, both at undergraduate and postgraduate levels, while ever more academics have turned their attention to the subject, either as a specialist area or within their own disciplinary 'home'.

It is, then, a popular but relatively young subject, and one that remains contentious. The press, for example, often refer to travel and tourism courses in rather disparaging terms while tourism academics themselves often indulge in a form of academic navel-gazing! At the same time, there is disagreement about the reason for studying travel and tourism. On the one hand, it can be seen as a vocational subject, preparing students for a career in tourism – certainly, many travel and tourism graduates secure jobs in the industry once they have completed their degree. On the other hand, there are powerful reasons for studying it as an academic subject in its own right:

- Travel and tourism is often claimed to be the world's largest industry. Although it is debatable whether the term 'industry' is appropriate, there is no doubting the enormous global economic value of travel and tourism.
- It is a major social phenomenon. As ever-increasing numbers of people become tourists it is important to understand why and how people travel.
- Travel and tourism has significant economic, environmental and socio-cultural consequences for destinations. Not only must these be understood and managed, but also they should be considered within broader global change and development.
- More generally, travel and tourism is an integral part of modern life and, therefore, deserving of academic study.

Despite the ongoing debate about the reasons for studying it, there is general consensus about what the study of travel and tourism is all about. Tourism is, essentially, a social activity; it is about people travelling, for whatever reason, to destinations away from the place where they normally live and work, and their activities during their stay in those destinations. In short, tourism is simply about people who are tourists.

Similarly, the starting point for the *study* of travel and tourism is the tourist, or the social activity of tourism. It is through the process of travelling and staying in destinations that, collectively, tourists spend huge sums of money, making travel and tourism one of the world's largest economic sectors and, for many countries, a vital industry; it is through that process that tourists interact with local people and impact on the local environment; it is through that process that tourists seek satisfying experiences. Therefore, it is through studying and understanding that process that those who cater for tourists – the travel and tourism industry – can better (and profitably!) meet tourists' needs, that the widely publicised problems or impacts of tourism can be better managed, and that destinations can optimise the benefits from tourism.

In other words, the study of travel and tourism is concerned with exploring how, why and where people travel as tourists, how the travel industry can effectively and profitably cater for tourists, and how destinations can harness and manage tourism to their benefit.

As a subject of study, travel and tourism cannot be described as an academic discipline in the traditional sense of the word; rather, it is a subject area that draws on a variety of disciplines that collectively contribute to the overall picture of the subject. In other words, there are a number of ways, or lenses, through which we can look at travel and tourism, and each of these lenses represents a particular discipline which provides a theoretical framework for exploring the subject. Of course, the contribution of each discipline to the study of travel and tourism is important in its own right. For example, not only has sociology provided a basis for studying tourist motivation and behaviour, but sociologists themselves are fascinated by tourism as what they refer to as a 'social institution'. However, the trick is to recognise that each discipline is one piece in the overall jigsaw of travel and tourism. Tourist motivation is a popular and interesting topic, yet of greater importance is its relevance to understanding tourism marketing, product development, destination management and so on. Therefore, your success in studying the subject will depend partly on the extent to which you can draw on and relate your knowledge of particular topics to understanding travel and tourism as a whole.

> Inevitably, some topics in travel and tourism will interest you more than others. However, it's important to remember that all the topics on your course are taught for a purpose; they will contribute collectively to your knowledge and understanding of travel and tourism.

As academic interest in travel and tourism has grown over the years, so too has the number of different disciplines that have contributed to the development of a broad-based body of knowledge on the subject. In fact, Jafar Jafari (1989), a leading academic who established one of the first (and now the most respected) tourism academic journals, *Annals of Tourism Research*, suggests that it is only recently that a more complete, multidisciplinary understanding of travel and tourism has evolved. He identifies four stages, or platforms, upon which the study of tourism has been based:

1 *The advocacy platform*. International **mass tourism** began to increase rapidly from the early 1960s. At this time, tourism was seen primarily as an economic phenomenon, an expanding international business that, as an important source of income and employment, had the potential to generate economic growth in destination areas. Little concern was displayed for the possible impacts of tourism development and, consequently, the study of travel and tourism was focused principally on the **economic impacts** of tourism, including indicators such as the **multiplier effect**.

2 *The cautionary platform*. As international tourism grew in both scale and scope, so too did awareness of its negative consequences or impacts. As a result, academic attention turned increasingly towards the study of the **social, cultural** and **environmental impacts** of travel and tourism (still a fundamental element of most tourism courses), with a variety of disciplines, including anthropology, geography and sociology, contributing to the research. Questions were also raised about the role of travel and tourism in **international development**, with a number of key writers whose backgrounds were in development studies and political science arguing for a more cautious approach to the promotion of tourism.

3 *The adaptancy platform*. During the 1980s, as attention continued to focus on the negative impacts of mass tourism, a principal theme to emerge in the study of travel and tourism was that of **alternative tourism**, preparing the way for the emergence of the topic that was later to dominate tourism studies, namely, **sustainable tourism**. Alternative tourism was concerned with finding, literally, alternatives to mass tourism development that had been so roundly criticised from the 1970s onwards, although, according to some, this represented a somewhat idealistic period in the study of travel and tourism.

4 *The knowledge platform*. Since the early 1990s, contrasting with the more thematic preceding 'platforms', the study of travel and tourism has become more holistic and rounded, with a variety of disciplines contributing to a more complete knowledge and understanding of the subject.

There is no doubt then that, over the last fifteen years or so, the scope of the subject has expanded enormously, as evidenced by the rapidly growing number of books dealing with increasingly diverse yet specific issues in travel and tourism. Curiously, in fact, compared with other subjects there are few general travel and tourism textbooks but many that focus on specialist areas. These reflect the large number of topics that comprise travel and tourism, many of which are covered in Part Two of this Companion, and which point to the increasing complexity of the subject. Nevertheless, travel and tourism can be subdivided into a number of broad thematic areas, all of which are included, to a greater or lesser extent, on courses and which indicate the breadth of the subject you will be studying.

- The business of travel and tourism. This is a large topic and is concerned mainly with the supply of tourism or, more specifically, the **tourism industry**. It embraces the study of different sectors of the industry, such as transport, tour operations, attractions or accommodation, as well as functional elements of business and management as applied to travel and tourism, including marketing, strategic management, finance, quality management and human resource management. The legal aspects of tourism also fall under this heading, while e.commerce or **e.tourism** is a relatively new sub-theme.
- The demand for tourism. Understanding the demand for tourism, or the consumer behaviour of tourists, has long been a concern for academics and is fundamental to the study of travel and tourism. In addition to the analysis of actual trends and flows in travel and tourism, this topic also explores the **tourism demand process**, **tourist motivation**, the psychology of travel and tourism, **tourist typologies**, **consumer culture** and changes in the nature of demand.
- Forms of travel and tourism. Much of the study of travel and tourism focuses on different forms of tourism as related to specific destinational categories. In addition to considering specific factors, these inevitably embrace issues relevant to travel and tourism as a whole, such as demand, planning, marketing and development, but in the context of the particular destinations. These include the countryside (**rural tourism**), towns and cities (**urban tourism**), **island tourism** and **marine tourism**.
- Tourism products and markets. Typically, travel and tourism is seen in terms of 'the holiday'. However, a significant proportion of domestic and **international tourism** is related to non-leisure purposes, such as **business travel**, attending conferences/events, or education. Moreover, as both the demand for and supply of tourism has become more sophisticated, an increasing variety of travel and tourism experiences can be identified, such as **adventure tourism**, **sport tourism**, **dark tourism**, **wine tourism**, backpacker/**youth tourism**, **religious tourism** or, more generally, **special interest tourism**. As a result, increasing academic attention is being paid to these specific products and markets.
- Tourism, culture and heritage. The relationship between tourism, culture and heritage is a dominant theme in the study of travel and tourism. More specifically, academics have long been concerned with the consequences of

tourism development on destination cultures while, more recently, culture and heritage as a tourism product has become a popular topic. Increasingly, attention has also been paid to travel and tourism as a modern cultural phenomenon.

- Planning and managing travel and tourism. Perhaps the greatest challenge is the effective planning and management of tourism development to ensure that the benefits of travel and tourism are optimised (or the costs minimised) for all stakeholders – that is, for destination communities and environments, for the travel and tourism industry, and for tourists themselves. This broad thematic area includes, therefore, a variety of topics including tourism policy and planning, tourism impacts, tourism and regional/national development, destination or resort management, **tourism development models** (including sustainable tourism) and environmental management, as well as more specific topics such as **visitor management**.

By now, you will have realised that travel and tourism is a broad and complex subject, and perhaps more so than you might have initially imagined. However, it is this diversity that makes it such an interesting subject of study, as does the fact that we are all tourists and, therefore, part of what we are learning about. Moreover, travel and tourism itself is a fascinating, dynamic business, facing ever-new demands and challenges and, as a result, there is always something new to learn about it.

One question you might be asking, therefore, is how do you make sense of the subject? To put it another way, given the variety of disciplinary perspectives and the vast array of topics included in travel and tourism courses, how can a common thread be found or an overall

External influences: economic, political, environmental, technological

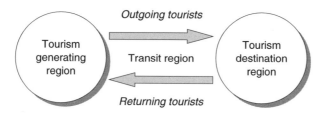

Outgoing tourists

Tourism generating region

Transit region

Tourism destination region

Returning tourists

Figure 1.1   Travel and tourism as a system

- The tourism generating region stimulates tourism and is where tour operators and travel agents are located.
- The tourism destination region attracts tourists, experiences the consequences of tourism and is where attractions and facilities, such as hotels, are located.
- The transit region represents the travel sector.

picture of the subject developed? The answer, perhaps, lies in a model of the **'tourism system'** first developed by Neil Leiper in the later 1970s. In this model, there are two main geographic regions, the tourism generating region and the tourism destination region, plus an intermediate transit route region (see Figure 1.1).

The three regions are, in a sense, linked by the tourist as the 'actor' in the system, while the system itself is subject to a number of external influences, such as political, economic or environmental factors, which determine the functioning of the system.

> *Thinking of travel and tourism as a system will help you to contextualise the individual topics you study, to understand how the different elements of tourism interact, and to relate specific issues to the subject as a whole. It will also remind you that travel and tourism cannot be seen in isolation from the world within which it occurs.*

Finally, the dynamic nature of travel and tourism represents both a challenge and an opportunity. It means that you should, ideally, keep up to date with what is happening in the 'real world' of travel and tourism, such as following developments in the airline industry or keeping up to date with the impact of the Internet on holiday purchasing, by regularly reading the trade press, newspapers and other sources of information. However, this will not only stimulate your interest in the subject but, perhaps more importantly, you are likely to impress your examiners! That is, the more you are able to relate the theory you are taught in lectures to appropriate examples of contemporary travel and tourism issues and practice, the more likely you are to succeed in your coursework and exams.

Running themes in travel and tourism

Despite the complex, multidisciplinary nature of travel and tourism, there are a number of themes which run across the subject as a whole. In a sense, these themes are the cement that binds the building blocks of the subject into a cohesive whole, and are relevant to most, if not all topics within travel and tourism. Try to bear them in mind when writing assignments or exam answers – they will help you to focus your ideas and arguments.

1 *Authenticity.* The concept of authentic tourist experiences has been a dominant theme in the study of travel and tourism since the 1970s, and is relevant to a variety of topics including marketing, destination planning and attraction management.

2 *Sustainable development.* The purpose of all tourism development is to achieve broader sustainable development in destination areas.

3 *Globalisation.* Travel and tourism contributes to, and is influenced by, the process of globalisation.

4 *Political economy.* National and international political and economic structures are inevitably linked with travel and tourism flows and development.

5 *The tourism industry.* Travel and tourism cannot occur without those who cater for tourists' needs, providing or facilitating tourism experiences.

6 *The tourism system.* All aspects of travel and tourism are interrelated within the concept of the tourism system.

7 *Sociology of tourism.* Travel and tourism is, first and foremost, a social phenomenon; a sociological understanding is fundamental to its effective planning and management.

8 *Governance.* It is always important to ask the question: who really determines tourism development policy?

You are probably aware that travel and tourism courses come in all shapes and sizes! A quick look at any guide to courses reveals a confusing list of different course names, from straight 'tourism' to 'tourism management', 'international tourism' or more specialist courses, such as 'sport tourism'. This diversity reflects the fact that not only is there is no travel and tourism curriculum as such, but also that different courses often have a specific focus or emphasis. This, in turn, may reflect the particular interests of your lecturers who, inevitably, have favourite topics or perspectives on tourism.

> *Just because a lecturer favours particular topics, theories or arguments does not mean you have agree to with them or repeat them in your assignments or exams! You will not lose marks (and will probably get better grades) for challenging or 'critiquing' what you have been taught, as long as you can justify your arguments.*

At the same time, new specialist units are constantly being developed as a result of lecturers' research interests or themes coming into fashion. However, most travel and tourism courses cover the same core topics to a lesser or greater extent, albeit frequently within differently named units or modules. For example, the impacts of tourism may be taught as a dedicated unit, or within broader units such as 'sustainable tourism' or 'destination management'.

These core topics are introduced in this part of the book. Each section provides you with a brief overview of the important issues, concepts and, where relevant, key writers on the subject, as well as a sample exam question and a guide to the issues you should include in your answers. Try to keep the running themes in mind and don't forget that travel and tourism is a 'real world' phenomenon – using contemporary examples will bring your answers to life.

> *In certain topics in travel and tourism there are key writers (and their theories or arguments) that your lecturer would expect you to be aware of. Always try to include them in to your assignments or exam answers.*

1
introducing travel and tourism

The study of travel and tourism inevitably begins with an overview of the subject as a modern social and economic phenomenon. Many textbooks begin by expressing its global significance in terms of **international tourist arrivals** and **international tourism receipts**, but three topics are of particular importance in introducing travel and tourism. These are, first, definitions, which attempt to clarify what travel and tourism is; second, the evolution of modern mass tourism, which explains how and why travel and tourism has become such a significant and widespread activity; and, third, the tourism system, which provides a framework for studying the subject.

Normally, attempts to define travel and tourism focus on the *demand* for tourism; definitions of the *supply* of travel and tourism are concerned with the nature and scope of the travel and tourism industry (see Section 4 below). It is, therefore, important to remember the sociology of tourism as a running theme here as the demand side of travel and tourism is concerned primarily with the tourist. There are two ways of attempting to define travel and tourism demand:

1 *Technical definitions*. Most commonly, definitions of travel and tourism are concerned with *who* is (or isn't) a tourist rather than *what* travel and tourism is. That is, they classify the tourist according to various criteria, such as length of stay, purpose of trip or distance travelled, and are used to distinguish tourism from other forms of travel for statistical or measurement purposes. Rather confusingly, distinctions are made between tourists, **'excursionists'** and **'day trippers'**; it is most useful to simply consider them all as tourists, remembering that day trips are usually a subcategory of **domestic tourism'**. The important point to grasp, however, is that tourism, as measured in numerous statistical sources, is a broad activity; tourists are not only people on holiday, but may be on business, students studying abroad, religious tourists (pilgrims), and so on.

2 *Conceptual definitions*. In contrast, these attempt to define the meaning or function of travel and tourism as a social activity. They draw attention to the fact that tourism involves a

change of location and, frequently, a change from the routine or the ordinary. However, given the enormous variety of purposes and activities measured as 'tourism', it is virtually impossible to define it conceptually – in fact, much of what you will cover on your course is concerned with what travel and tourism is.

Although it is useful to be able to quote the definitions you might find in textbooks, it is more important to recognise the contribution or limitations of different types of definition to an understanding of what travel and tourism is.

The evolution or history of tourism is a fascinating subject in its own right (and an example of how particular disciplines can contribute to our understanding of travel and tourism). Given the increasing incidence of travel and tourism in modern societies, it is also an important topic in the social history of many countries. The main purpose of looking at how travel and tourism has evolved, however, is to identify the main factors that have influenced, and continue to drive, the growth and spread of tourism around the world. Thus, if you are investigating the growth of travel and tourism either generally or in specific countries/regions, it is likely that you will always be able to refer to these factors.

The principal issue to focus upon is the transformation of travel and tourism, particularly international travel and tourism, from an activity that was once largely the preserve of the privileged minority (the wealthy or upper classes) to one enjoyed by the great majority of people, at least in the wealthier, developed countries. In other words, the principal issue is the emergence of mass tourism, a process that is described by one key writer, John Urry, as the 'democratisation' of tourism. The main question to think about is, how has this **democratisation of tourism** come about?

On the one hand, an historical analysis of tourism development identifies three main periods within which specific forms of tourism can be identified:

1 *1600–1800:* a period which witnessed the rise and fall of the '**Grand Tour**', as well as the popularity of spas as the first example of resort-based tourism.

2 *1800–1900:* during this period, seaside resorts emerged and grew rapidly. The latter half of the 19th century also saw the birth and development of the '**package tour**', with Thomas Cook being widely considered as the originator of the concept.

3 *1900 onwards:* a period initially defined by increasing domestic tourism but, since the 1960s, by the rapid growth of inter-national mass tourism.

Importantly, a common theme or trend throughout all these periods, and one that continues to reflect the development of contemporary travel and tourism, is the so-called 'aristocratic model' of tourism development. The upper classes or aristocracy initially favoured particular destinations or types of tourism, only to find their leisure space and time being increasingly invaded by the middle/lower classes or less well-to-do. In other words, travel and tourism has long been a status symbol and one to which people increasingly aspire. This can be used to explain many current trends in tourism – bear this in mind when you are studying tourism demand or the consumption of tourism.

On the other hand, the democratisation of tourism can be explained by a number of key drivers that have underpinned the growth of mass tourism. In particular, four factors, all of which deserve to be explored in some detail, have contributed to this process:

1 *Technological developments.* Advances in transport technology have been fundamental to the growth in travel and tourism, both in increasing peoples' access to various forms of transport and in extending the distance that they can travel. More recently, information technology has also facilitated the growth in travel and tourism.

2 *Increases in personal wealth and time.* Quite evidently, people require sufficient amounts of both money and free time to participate in travel and tourism.

3 *Social transformations.* Social, economic and political change continues to be an important factor in the encouragement of travel and tourism.

4 *The emergence of a sophisticated travel industry.* While travel and tourism is, essentially, a social phenomenon, its growth has been dependent upon an expanding, integrated and innovative industry catering to (and, perhaps, creating) tourists' needs.

The history of travel and tourism has not yet run its course. New destinations, generating regions, products and markets are constantly evolving and these can be explained or even predicted by referring to the factors that have historically influenced the evolution of tourism.

A simple way of thinking about travel and tourism is that it comprises three basic elements:

1 *Tourists:* their demands, expectations, motivations and behaviour.

2 *The destination:* where the tourist experience occurs and where the benefits and costs of tourism development are felt.

3 *The travel and tourism industry:* innumerable businesses and organisations that collectively cater for the needs of tourists.

Although these are often studied as independent topics, in reality they are anything but independent. Indeed, one of the defining characteristics of tourism is that, for destinations, it is an export industry – the destination is the 'product' that is sold to overseas customers (or, in the case of domestic tourism, to visitors from other regions). Uniquely, that product is consumed where it is produced, pointing to an interrelationship between the destination, tourists and the travel industry which, frequently, both carries tourists to and provides for their needs within the destination. Thus, travel and tourism can be thought of as an interrelated system.

Reference has already been made in the first part of this book to the model of the tourism system developed by Neil Lieper (see Figure 1.1). There are three elements of this system:

1 *Tourists.* Tourism is, first and foremost, a human activity and it is around the tourist and tourism experiences that the model is built.

2 *Geographical areas.* There are three constituent regions in tourism – the generating region, where tourists come from, the destination region, where they travel to and stay, and an intermediate transit region, which represents both travel to the destination and short stays en route. Each of these regions is interrelated with tourists and the tourism industry.

3 *The travel and tourism industry.* The businesses and organisations which cater for tourists' needs can be located in each of the three regions.

The benefit of the tourism system model is that it provides a particular way of looking at travel and tourism, both generally and in the context of specific forms of tourism. Thus, specific destinations or types of tourism development, such as **ecotourism**, can be analysed within the model. It also provides a unifying framework for exploring and understanding the interaction between all the stakeholders in travel and tourism.

> *The model of the tourism system is just that – a model. While it is useful to understand it as a concept, its real value lies in its application as a framework for analysing specific tourism contexts or issues.*

Taking it *FURTHER*

Most travel and tourism courses and textbooks typically begin by addressing the question: what is tourism? They then go on to consider the different definitions of tourism and highlight the diversity of tourist types. Beyond technically defining tourism for measurement purposes, however, is there any value in attempting to define it? Or, is it actually possible to define it? Travel and tourism has become an ubiquitous part of modern life, something that most of us do in some form or another. It has, in a sense, become a mass phenomenon, an activity in which the masses participate. Does this then imply that we are all, in effect, mass tourists?

Exam questions related to introductory sessions in travel and tourism are most likely to focus on two of the three themes outlined here: definitions, and the evolution of travel and tourism. A typical 'definitions' question would be:

"Why is it difficult to define travel and tourism succinctly?"

At a basic level, this requires you to demonstrate your knowledge of the different definitions of travel and tourism, in particular the distinction between and contributions of the demand/supply side and technical/conceptual definitions. Reference to the diverse categories of tourist would also be expected. However, the question also demands a more critical analysis of what tourism is as a social activity, its democratisation and its subsequent position in modern, social life. Indeed, so ingrained is travel and tourism in modern societies that there is, perhaps, little point in trying to define it other than for technical measurement purposes related to its volume and economic value.

A simple, 'evolution' question might ask:

❝ What have been the key factors in the development of modern mass tourism? ❞

The evolution of travel and tourism can be explored by referring descriptively to particular periods, the specific types of tourism that were popular during those periods, and the common factors across all periods (technology, time/money, social change and the influence of the travel and tourism industry). It is important to consider how these continue to drive the growth of travel and tourism, and also to assess the relative influence of each. For example, the travel industry has been a dominant force in creating, as well as satisfying, the demand for tourism while, more recently, developments in ICT (Information and Communication Technology) have significantly influenced how people purchase tourism products.

Textbook guide

COOPER ET AL. (2005): *Chapter 1*
HOLLOWAY (2002): *Chapters 1 to 3*
SHARPLEY (2002): *Chapters 1 and 2*
SHAW AND WILLIAMS (2002): *Chapter 1*

2

global tourism

Travel and tourism is a global phenomenon. Not only is it one of the world's largest economic sectors but also the so-called '**pleasure** periphery' (a useful term to describe the extent of international leisure travel) has embraced the entire world. That is, few, if any, countries are not now part of the tourism system. At the same time, travel and tourism is inextricably linked to (the running theme of) globalisation, a process that tourism both contributes to and is influenced by.

At a basic level, then, global tourism is seen in terms of its scale and scope which, typically, are measured in terms of international tourist arrivals and international receipts, either by country, region or globally. Detailed data are available for most countries, indicating annual arrivals, receipts and growth trends. The **World Tourism Organization** (WTO) is an invaluable source of information. In addition to comprehensive volumes of statistics published annually, a summary of the most recent data, *Tourism Highlights*, can be downloaded from the WTO website (www.world-tourism.org/facts/eng/highlights.htm). The **World Travel and Tourism Council** (WTTC) is also a good source of information. Their country **tourism satellite accounts** and league tables are well worth looking at.

Always try to use the most recent data in your assignments and exams. While WTO and WTTC statistics are reasonably contemporary (and in many cases the only sources of reliable data), you may find that information published by a particular country's national tourism organisation – often to be found on the Internet – is the most up to date.

However, two things should be considered generally when thinking about global travel and tourism:

1 It is not only about international travel and tourism. Globally, the majority of tourist trips are *within* national borders; it is estimated that, worldwide, domestic tourism is, in terms of volume, between six and ten times greater than international travel and tourism. It is, however, much more difficult to measure than international tourism.

2 A number of issues are most relevant at the global level, such as the role of tourism in development, tourism and the environment/**sustainable tourism development**, and so-called barriers to travel and tourism (natural disasters, terrorism, etc.).

The key themes within the study of global tourism build upon the descriptive data relating to tourist flows and receipts, and are concerned primarily with analysing and explaining trends and transformations in the overall worldwide picture of travel and tourism. The tourism system model provides a useful framework for exploring these trends in terms of both the relationship between generating and destination regions and of the influence of external factors on parts of the system or on the system as a whole. Evidently, therefore, national and international political economy is also an important running theme to consider here.

> *As interesting (and impressive!) as many of the global travel and tourism statistics are in their own right, it is important to look beyond the actual figures to explore the reasons for trends and changes, and to assess the implications of those trends and changes for international tourism destinations and the travel and tourism industry.*

The trends and transformations in global travel and tourism can be assessed at different, but interrelated, geographic levels: the global, the regional and the national. In fact, most textbooks cover what is usually referred to as the 'geography of travel and tourism' at these three levels. Similarly, the WTO provides detailed national data for most tourism receiving countries but assesses their implication in both global terms and according to six (somewhat arbitrary) international regions. Each level of analysis tells us a different 'story'; however, not only are there themes common to each but also they contribute collectively to an overall picture of global travel and tourism.

The global level

Most commonly, a global perspective on travel and tourism focuses upon two key issues:

1 The worldwide scale and value of travel and tourism. Over the last half century, international travel and tourism has grown dramatically in terms of both arrivals and receipts. However, the key point is that, although the annual rate of growth is slowing, travel and tourism is resilient to external factors. Major events, such as '9/11', have only limited and temporary impacts on overall growth of travel and tourism, which is forecast to continue in the foreseeable future.

2 The contribution of travel and tourism to the global economy. The most powerful justification for developing tourism is its contribution to national, regional and global GDP and employment.

When assessing actual and predicted growth in travel and tourism worldwide, it is important to think about the implications of this growth with respect to environmental concerns, infrastructural needs (for example, airports), safety issues, and so on.

However, it is also important to recognise the global patterns of travel and tourism flows/trends and the reasons for them. Specifically, travel and tourism flows are not equitable (or equally enjoyed by all regions or countries); they tend to be regionalised (i.e. within particular regions) and polarised (i.e. between particular countries). These patterns are, to an extent, influenced by the historical 'drivers' of the growth in travel and tourism (see Section 1), but global tourist flows are also determined by:

- the nature and supply of tourism resources (natural, man-made, cultural) at the global and national scales
- distance between destinations and main generating regions
- transport and communication networks
- climate and climate change
- national and international political economy
- globalisation of the world economy and business.

The regional scale

As noted, travel and tourism flows are highly regionalised; that is, the most significant flows of international tourism occur within particular regions. At the same time, the WTO divides the world into six regions for the purpose of comparison and analysis, while some regions also have their own regional (for example, **PATA, CTO**) or sub-regional tourism organisations which collate and disseminate information, develop regional tourism policies, and so on. Moreover, many external influences (wars, terrorism, health scares, etc.) are most keenly felt at the regional level. Therefore, a regional perspective on global travel and tourism is concerned with:

- an analysis of the volume, value and growth trends of travel and tourism *within* regions, the potential for future growth, and regional policies, and
- comparisons *between* regions. This is the principal means of identifying and explaining transformations in the patterns of international tourism flows.

All regions or countries compete for tourist arrivals within the global travel and tourism market. Comparing the volume and value of travel and tourism at the regional level reveals how each region's share of global tourism is increasing or decreasing. This is an important factor when looking at tourism policy/planning at the national or regional level.

The national levels

Travel and tourism statistics relating to individual countries are usually compiled into annual league tables of the world's leading tourism generating countries (either by departures or spending) and tourism destination countries (either by the number of arrivals or tourism receipts). These provide, of course, an indication of how each country is performing relative to other tourism destinations (that is, their share of global travel and tourism) as well as providing a more detailed picture of the shifting patterns of tourism flows.

However, at the national level it is also vital to consider the volume/value of travel and tourism relative to other national criteria, such as employment or contribution to GDP. In other words, global league tables of international tourist arrivals/receipts tend to disguise the varying importance of travel and tourism to different countries. For example, the size and value of the travel and tourism sector in many **least developed countries** is insignificant in global terms but is often the largest economic sector within the country. Therefore, when countries are listed according to the importance of tourism to the national economy, a very different picture of global tourism emerges. The WTTC's country league tables, accessible on the WTTC website, provide much of the information you might require.

While international tourism arrivals and receipts data provide a basic picture of global travel and tourism flows and trends, you can add an extra dimension to your analysis by exploring different measures of the importance of tourism to destinations, such as its contribution to exports, national income or employment.

Barriers to travel and tourism

It is evident from the tourism system model that a variety of external influences or forces impact upon the functioning of the system, particularly the nature and direction of tourist flows. Any analysis of global tourism should identify and explore the implications of these 'barriers', wherever possible using appropriate examples. The following are categories of **barriers to travel and tourism** from which you can draw specific examples:

- government intervention/policies
- political instability
- economic instability
- conflict
- crime
- health scares
- natural disasters.

Taking it *FURTHER*

There are numerous sources of data that measure the scale and value of international travel and tourism, more often than not compiled into global league tables. More specifically, the statistics are frequently used to identify the world's principal destination countries or regions, the main generating countries, and trends/changes in these. However, how appropriate is it to compare different (WTO-defined) regions rather than limiting the comparison to different countries? Moreover, most data focus on tourist arrivals and receipts, but are these the most useful basis for measuring or comparing the value or importance of global travel and tourism? In other words, flows and trends in global tourism are more than adequately described by travel and tourism statistics, but a more accurate picture of the importance of travel and tourism is likely to emerge from comparisons of in-depth national analyses.

When looking at global travel and tourism, in particular international tourism trends and flows, exam questions will normally require you to demonstrate both your knowledge of contemporary patterns of travel and tourism, and your understanding of the factors that determine these patterns. A typical question might be:

"How are international tourism flows changing and why?"

The main feature of global tourism in recent years has been the decline in Europe's domination of international tourism and the increasing share of international arrivals and receipts enjoyed by the Middle East and East Asia and Pacific (EAP) regions. Growth in these areas has been driven by a variety of factors, principally an increase in intra-regional travel based on increasing regional wealth and the business development around the Pacific Rim, but has also been affected by a number of major external events, such as terrorism, the Asian financial crisis and the SARS outbreak. However, some of the most significant growth in tourism has been achieved by small, less developed countries which are attracting increasing numbers of visitors from the main generating regions.

Alternatively, you may be asked:

❝ Why is it that certain regions of the world are unlikely to gain a major share of international tourist flows? ❞

The traditional dominance of Europe in international tourism can be explained by a number of factors, including freedom of movement across borders, a large supply of attractions and facilities, relatively short distances between generating and destination regions, and established transport and communication links. Referring to these factors, your answer should explore the extent to which these are lacking in some parts of world, exacerbated by a number of barriers which may prohibit the development of tourism.

Textbook guide

BONIFACE AND COOPER **(2001):** *Chapters 1 to 5*
BURTON **(1995):** *Chapters 15 to 17*
SHARPLEY **(2002):** *Chapter 3*
SHAW AND WILLIAMS **(2002):** *Chapter 2*

3

the demand for travel and tourism

Travel and tourism starts with the tourist – if people did not wish to be tourists or to seek out tourism experiences, travel and tourism would, by and large, not be the major phenomenon it is today. Therefore, understanding why people want or choose to be tourists is fundamental to the study of travel and tourism.

The demand for tourism is, however, a broad topic. It is not only about how and why people decide to participate in tourism, but also about how they behave as tourists, why they choose particular types of tourism, what tourism means to them, why their 'taste' in tourism may change over time, and so on. In short, to study the demand for travel and tourism is, in effect, to study the tourist. Inevitably, then, it is one of the largest (and most researched or written about) topics within the study of travel and tourism and, perhaps, one of the most complex. It also draws on a number of the social sciences, particularly sociology, anthropology and psychology, while key running themes are the sociology of tourism and authenticity. Nevertheless, the basic principles and concepts within the demand for travel and tourism are relatively simple and, once you have grasped these, then you will be much better placed to explore areas of particular interest in more detail.

To start, it is vital to understand what is meant by 'demand' – a common mistake, for example, is to equate 'demand' with 'motivation' but, as we shall see, demand is the *outcome* of motivation. There are three kinds of demand:

1 *Actual/expressed demand*: the actual number of people who participate in travel and tourism, as measured in tourism statistics.

2 *Suppressed demand*: potential tourists who would travel if their personal circumstances allowed it.

3 *Latent demand:* potential tourists whose needs cannot be met by particular destinations/products.

When studying the demand for travel and tourism, we are principally concerned with actual or expressed demand. Two further points are worth remembering. First, for many people, tourism demand is a continuous, cyclical process – the experience and memory from one holiday often feeds the anticipation and experience of the next one. Second, the demand for travel and tourism needs to be considered alongside all other forms of consumption that we indulge in – it is just one element of our general consumer behaviour.

> *When reading or thinking about tourism demand, try to relate particular concepts or theoretical processes to your own experience as a tourist. This will help you to understand and 'critique' what you are reading.*

A useful framework for studying/understanding travel and tourism demand is provided by the tourism demand process. You will find different models of this process in most textbooks, though they are all based upon a generic model of consumer decision-making made up of five stages:

Stage 1   Problem identification/'felt need'
Stage 2   Information search and evaluation
Stage 3   Purchase (travel) decision
Stage 4   Travel experience
Stage 5   Experience evaluation.

Inevitably this oversimplifies a complex process. Each stage is subject to a variety of influences and factors (see Figure 2.1 as an example), while the concept of the **travel career ladder** also adds an extra dimension.

> *While models of the demand process are useful to bear in mind, it is the enormous variety of factors that may influence each and every stage of the process that is fundamental to understanding the demand for travel and tourism.*

These factors can be usefully categorised under four headings, as suggested by Cooper et al. (2005). These will also help you to clarify and contextualise different concepts that are often applied to the demand for travel and tourism.

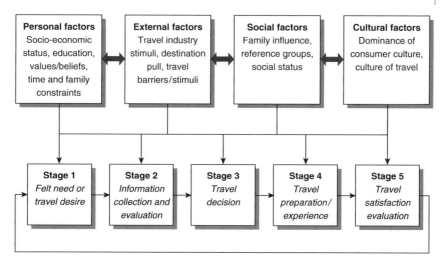

Figure 2.1   The tourism demand process

1 *Energisers of demand.* These are the forces and influences that collectively create the motivation to travel or go on holiday. They are the **push factors** which initiate the demand process (i.e Stage 1). The next section of the book (Section 4) deals exclusively with tourist motivation.

2 *Effectors of demand.* The information search/evaluation process and subsequent purchase decisions (i.e. Stages 2 and 3) are influenced by the tourist's knowledge and perceptions of particular places, destinations or experiences. These are the **pull factors** which lead the tourist to making particular travel choices.

3 *Filterers/determinants of demand.* A variety of economic, social and psychological factors determine particular choices or 'filter out' inappropriate products. These include tangible or descriptive demand factors, such as:

- mobility
- employment and income
- paid holiday entitlement
- education levels
- demographic variables: age, gender, race, stage in the family life cycle.

To an extent, the above factors are useful for **market segmentation** and as a basic predictor of what choices particular consumer groups will make. However, the decision-making process is also influenced by intangible, or lifestyle factors, sometimes referred to as psychographic variables. All individuals possess values, attitudes and beliefs which guide their behaviour or determine their lifestyle. The **VALS** (Values and Lifestyle Scale) is a useful model to apply to travel and tourism.

4 *Roles.* Holiday/travel choices are also influenced by roles both within the purchasing 'unit' (for example, the different roles adopted by family members in choosing a holiday) and as tourists. With regards to the latter, tourists play roles (or see themselves as playing such roles) which may determine their travel/holiday choices. A number of writers have attempted to categorise these roles into tourist typologies, some focusing on tourists' psychographic characteristics, such as Plog's **psychocentric–allocentric** continuum model, others on the relationship between tourist types and the destination environment. The most significant (and widely cited) contribution is that of Erik Cohen, who bases his typologies on the idea that tourists are more or less willing/able to seek out either the familiar or the novel/different and can, therefore, be categorised along a continuum, from the 'organised mass tourist' at one end to the 'drifter' at the other.

Tourist typologies describe and potentially explain certain tourist roles; however, they tend to over-generalise tourist behaviour and overlook the myriad of other factors that influence the demand for travel and tourism. Therefore, they should not be seen as predictors of tourist behaviour.

Changes in demand

In addition to understanding the nature of and influences on the tourism demand process, it is important to think about how the overall demand for travel and tourism is changing (and why). You need to be aware of two interrelated themes:

1 *The production–consumption relationship.* So-called **Fordist production** required consumers to accept mass-produced products, as in the early forms of mass package tourism. In the

post-Fordist era, manufacturers or producers are obliged to respond to frequent changes in taste and fashion.

2 *The 'new' tourist.* It is claimed that tourists are becoming more adventurous, flexible, environmentally aware, active and discerning, and are seeking greater quality, variety and value for money.

As evidence of these, a variety of trends in demand can be observed, such as the growth of the ecotourism market, expansion of the long-haul market, growth in the short-break market and the increasing domination of independent, as opposed to organised (package) holidays. Nevertheless, it is important to question the concept of the 'new tourist' – have we changed that much in our holidaying habits?

Taking it *FURTHER*

Models of the travel and tourism demand process imply that tourists, as consumers, follow a logical, rational process. They also suggest that, if particular factors and influences can be identified, then it is possible to predict how certain groups or types of tourist will behave in terms of making travel or holiday decisions. However, most forms of consumption (and travel and tourism in particular) are neither logical nor rational, and such is the diversity of factors that determine people's buying decisions that is virtually impossible to categorise tourists or predict their behaviour. Moreover, people are increasingly taking multiple holidays of different types each year. It is, then, worthwhile exploring the concept of the **post-tourist** and, consequently, the extent to which tourism demand models and tourist typologies have become largely irrelevant.

Given the breadth of the topic, exam questions on the demand for travel and tourism can vary enormously. You may be asked to critically appraise particular concepts, such as tourist typologies, to consider the extent to which the 'new tourist' is manifested in practice, or to assess the tourism demand process from the perspective of the travel and tourism industry. Generally, however, questions are likely to focus on your understanding of the factors that determine the decision-making process and its overall contribution to predicting consumer behaviour in travel and tourism. Therefore, a typical exam question might be:

❝ How effective are models of the tourism demand process in predicting the demand for travel and tourism? ❞

This question would require you to identify different demand models and to discuss the variety of factors (under headings such as energisers, effectors, roles and determinants) that influence the decision-making process. The extent to which tourism demand can be predicted by such models could then be appraised by looking at contemporary trends in tourism demand and/or by considering the different factors that might stimulate demand for a particular destination.

An alternative question might focus on the psychographic variables that may influence the demand for tourism:

❝ How relevant are an individual's values to the tourism decision-making process? ❞

All individuals possess values which determine their behaviour and lifestyle. These values may be instrumental, or a means of achieving a desired outcome, or ends in themselves. Moreover, an individual's values usually form a hierarchy – some are more important than others. After reviewing the role of values in determining behaviour, your answer would explore particular values that may influence tourism buying decisions, concluding that much depends on individual values and the importance they place on them.

Finally, you may be asked a conceptual question, such as:

❝ How relevant are tourist typologies in the era of the 'post-tourist'? ❞

Tourist typologies, in categorising tourists according to a variety of criteria, attempt to explain different modes of tourist behaviour. Conversely, the concept of the post-tourist suggests that tourists have come of age; they understand that tourism is a kind of game, that there is huge choice in tourism and that they can enjoy that choice. Thus, a post-tourist defies categorisation, playing the role of all the different tourist types within a particular typology.

4	
tourist motivation	

The previous section looked at travel and tourism demand in general. In this section we now turn to a specific part of the demand process: tourist motivation. Motivation is the most important but, at the same time, most complex element of tourism demand. On the one hand, it has been described as one of the most basic and indispensable subjects in tourism studies – without motivation, there would be no demand for tourism. On the other hand, a complete understanding of the motivation for travel and tourism remains elusive. Indeed, one well-known writer, Jost Krippendorf, notes that most tourists themselves are unaware of what motivates them, making it even harder for academics to research the subject. Nevertheless, adopting a structured way of looking at tourist motivation will help you to chart a path through the numerous, and sometimes confusing, books, chapters and articles on the topic.

It is essential to grasp some basic principles about tourist motivation:

- Motivation is not the same as demand. The demand for travel and tourism is the outcome of motivation. A useful way to think of motivation is that it is the link between a 'felt need' (as in Stage 1 of the demand process) and the action needed or chosen to satisfy that need. Therefore, motivation translates an identified or felt need into goal-oriented consumer behaviour. Consequently, travel and tourism is a satisfier of needs and wants.

> *The simplest way to think about the role of motivation is to view it as the trigger that sets off the travel and tourism demand process; in a sense, motivation represents tourism's starting gun.*

- Motivation should not be equated with the purpose of a trip/holiday. More often than not, the purpose (getting a sun tan, learning about a new culture and so on) is a means of satisfying a particular need.
- Motivational push (i.e. person-specific needs) should not be confused with destinational pull (i.e. destination-specific attractors).
- The study of tourist motivation is, essentially, concerned with exploring why people feel the need to be tourists in the first place and how different needs may be satisfied by different tourism experiences.

Academics have long been interested in the topic of tourist motivation and have adopted a number of different approaches. An article by Graham Dann, which is summarised in many textbooks, reviews these approaches. However, there are two key ways of looking at motivation which reflect two disciplinary perspectives (psychology and sociology) on the subject: (i) motivation as a psychological phenomenon, and (ii) motivation as a sociological phenomenon.

Motivation as a psychological phenomenon (intrinsic motivation)

Every individual has deep-rooted needs and desires. This approach is concerned with establishing a link between such psychological needs and identified, goal-oriented touristic behaviour. Most commonly, Abraham Maslow's 'hierarchy of needs' is referred to in this context.

> *Although the attraction of Maslow's model lies in its simplicity (and many travel and tourism textbooks describe it), it contributes only partially to an understanding of tourist motivation. While not overlooking it completely, try to avoid focusing on it too much in your assignments or exam answers.*

Given the difficulty that tourists themselves have in recognising what motivates them, identifying psychological motives is a difficult task. Nevertheless, academics from both disciplinary 'camps' agree that **ego-enhancement** is an overall intrinsic need that may be satisfied by travel and tourism. Other such needs, sometimes referred to as a 'hidden agenda', include:

- escape/avoidance
- self-evaluation or realisation
- regression/freedom
- relaxation
- enhancement of relationships.

Motivation as a social/sociological phenomenon (extrinsic motivation)

There are a variety of forces or pressures arising from an individual's social and cultural environment which may influence his or her needs and motivation. Such external or extrinsic pressures may come from family and friends, the work environment, or society in general – for example, it is worth thinking about the extent to which we go on holiday simply because it is what we do (or what is expected of us) in contemporary society. The important point is that, although these influences are, in a sense, internalised and become personal needs, they originate in an individual's social environment. Therefore, the sociology of tourism is a vital running theme here, as is the specific theme of authenticity.

> *Both sociology and psychology contribute to an understanding of tourist motivation – the two perspectives complement each other. However, it is important to recognise, in particular, the variety of social and cultural influences that potentially influence tourists' motives.*

Extrinsic tourist motivation can be viewed from the point of view of the individual (a social action perspective) or as emanating from society as a whole (a structural/functionalist perspective). There are a number of influences (discussed below) that you need to be aware of as a basis for exploring extrinsic motivation.

The work–tourism relationship

Since the industrialisation/urbanisation of society, leisure in general, and travel and tourism in particular, have become the antithesis to work. Work is, therefore, a primary extrinsic motivational factor, the nature of the work experience often determining the desired tourism experience.

> *The work–tourism relationship is not only relevant to paid employment; 'work' should be considered as any form of obligatory or non-discretionary routine activity.*

The work–tourism relationship can take three forms:

- Work and tourism in opposition (the compensatory model). The concepts of **inversion, regression** and **ludic** behaviour are relevant here.
- Tourism as an extension of work.
- Neutrality between work and tourism.

Social influences

Tourist motivation is undoubtedly influenced by an individual's immediate and wider social group. There are four sources of social pressure:

- family influences
- reference groups
- social class
- culture.

> *None of the social influences on tourist motivation are mutually exclusive. While different influences may predominate at different times, they may also be linked to the work–tourism relationship. For example, social class and reference groups may be related to the nature of work. Therefore, it is useful to see them as contributing collectively to an understanding of tourist motivation.*

Modern society

A paradox of modern society is that not only has it provided the opportunity for travel and tourism (wealth, time, technology, etc.), but also that it has created the need for tourism. A primary motivational factor is the need to escape, albeit temporarily, from modern society. Therefore, from a functionalist perspective, travel and tourism plays an essential role in modern society by keeping it, in a sense, in good working order.

Key to understanding the motivational push of modern society are the concepts of **alienation** and **anomie**. As well as wishing to escape from the pressures and stress of modern life, it is claimed that tourists are seeking meaning and **authenticity** through travel and tourism. According to Dean MacCannell, a key writer on the subject, tourists are modern pilgrims seeking authentic experiences, yet are ultimately frustrated in that search as a result of **staged authenticity**.

A parallel theme in this context is the notion of travel and tourism representing a modern, spiritual experience or sacred journey. That is, it is seen as the modern equivalent of religious or sacred activities that people traditionally used to add sense or meaning to their lives. Fundamental to this is the linking of contemporary tourism with pilgrimage, with both the journey out/back and the stay at the destination (in a condition of **liminality**) being equated with the traditional pilgrimage experience.

Try not to confuse religious tourism (tourism that is motivated exclusively or partly by faith or religious reasons) with the idea of 'tourism as religion'. Visiting a holy or sacred site does not mean you are a religious tourist; conversely, you do not necessarily have to visit a holy or sacred site to be a religious tourist.

Taking it **FURTHER**

Tourist motivation is a highly complex issue and one which academics have long been concerned with. The various models and perspectives for studying the topic point to a range of forces and influences, both psychological and social, that may to a lesser or greater extent determine our needs and wants and, consequently, the type of tourist experience that we seek out. However, a full understanding of the topic remains elusive. For example, travel and tourism, from a demand perspective, is a continual process, the previous trip or holiday extending into memory and subsequent anticipation of the next one. To what extent, therefore, is demand driven by anticipation? Is looking forward to a holiday as important and beneficial as the holiday itself? It is also important to think about travel and tourism within a broader consumer culture context – there is as much to learn about *how* tourists 'consume' tourism as *why*.

Any exam question related to tourist motivation will provide you with the opportunity to demonstrate your knowledge of, first, the relevance of motivation to the overall tourism demand process and, second, the contribution of different perspectives on tourist motivation to understanding the phenomenon. You may well also be asked to consider tourist motivation in the context of particular types of tourism or different destinations. For example, you may be asked the following question:

"Why are tourists being increasingly motivated to participate in adventure tourism?"

Adventure tourism signifies challenge, risk, excitement, physical activity and a change from the ordinary. Each of these experiences may satisfy a different set of needs on the part of the tourist – compensation for a mundane job, the desire for a healthy lifestyle, the personal challenge, social interaction through sharing risky experiences with others, the enhanced social status of taking such a holiday, or simply following fashion. Your answer would explore how these different needs might be determined but, perhaps, concluding that it is the broader nature of modern society that is the dominant factor.

Conversely, questions may focus on a more general aspect of motivation, such as:

"Critically appraise the extent to which tourists are primarily motivated by the desire to escape."

Here, you would be expected to review the main perspectives on tourism motivation, highlighting the key factors that may influence or determine an individual's needs. Inherent in many motives, such as freedom, relaxation and so on, is the desire to escape from the physical and social structures of home life. At the same time, however, other motives collectively represent 'ego-enhancement' and, therefore, most tourists are likely to be motivated by a combination of escape and ego-enhancement.

Textbook guide

BURNS AND HOLDEN (1995): *Chapter 2*
COOPER ET AL. (2005): *Chapter 2*
HOLLOWAY (2002): *Chapter 5*
RYAN (2003): *Chapters 3 and 4*
SHARPLEY (2003): *Chapter 5*
SWARBROOKE AND HORNER (1999): *Chapter 4*

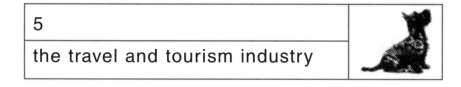

5
the travel and tourism industry

When studying the travel and tourism industry, you will normally find either that the relevant module/unit looks at each sector of the industry in turn or, as is often the case, that entire modules might be devoted to specific sectors. It is not unusual, for example, for travel and tourism courses to include separate modules on transport, accommodation/ hospitality, tour operations or attractions management. Either way, however, it is important that you are aware of certain concepts and debates about the nature and characteristics of the travel and tourism industry – these will provide you with a framework for looking at the constituent elements of the industry in more detail.

The travel and tourism industry is not only an important subject in its own right; it is also a theme that runs throughout the study of tourism and that is directly or indirectly relevant to virtually every area of the subject. Furthermore, it links to other running themes, such as governance, political economy, the tourism system and sustainable development. So, whatever area of travel and tourism you are looking at, always try to think of the importance or relevance of the industry.

The purpose of this section, then, is to provide that introductory framework while subsequent sections look at different sectors in more detail.

There are four key issues or questions that you need to bear in mind when thinking about the travel and tourism industry:

1 What is the travel and tourism industry?

2 What are the constituent sectors or elements of the industry?

3 How are these sectors related?

4 What is the 'product' of the travel and tourism industry?

What is the travel and tourism industry?

Although most textbooks refer to the 'travel and tourism industry', they tend to gloss over the rather thorny question of what is the industry or, more precisely, whether it can actually be described as an industry. Generally, the travel and tourism industry is considered to be all the individuals, businesses and organisations that, collectively, provide the products, services and, hence, overall experiences that tourists 'consume' or enjoy – it facilitates people's participation in tourism. It has a number of important characteristics:

- It is highly diverse. An enormous variety of businesses and organisations comprise the industry.
- Most travel and tourism businesses are **SME**s. Though we immediately think of large, international corporations, the majority of tourism organisations are, in fact, small and often family-run businesses.
- It is highly fragmented. There is little cohesion or coordination throughout the industry.
- It is private-sector dominated. Most businesses are motivated by short-term profit.

The vital point to remember is that, given its characteristics, the travel and tourism industry as a whole is difficult, if not impossible, to manage or control. This has significant implications for tourism policy and planning, as well as more specific concerns such as destination development and sustainable tourism development.

These characteristics also fuel the argument that it is misleading to describe travel and tourism as an industry. In fact, bearing in mind that, unlike other identifiable industries, there are no clear inputs, methods of production, chains of supply or outputs, it becomes difficult to see how travel and tourism is an 'industry'. Other points to remember include:

- Many sectors of travel and tourism are industries in their own right.
- Some tourism products and services (for example finance, insurance, guide books, and so on) are provided by businesses that are quite evidently not travel and tourism organisations.
- Many organisations are in either the public or voluntary (not-for-profit) sectors and may or not view travel and tourism as a primary purpose.
- There is no management structure or trade body for the 'industry' as a whole.

The most useful way of looking at travel and tourism is to think of it as a production system, the characteristics of which may vary according to particular destinations, countries or travel and tourism markets.

What are the constituent sectors or elements of the industry?

The key issue to bear in mind when considering the structure of the travel and tourism industry is its scope. While the most visible sectors are hotels, transport operators, travel retailers and attractions, a great number and variety of other organisations from the public and voluntary sectors (at the global, regional, national and local levels) also contribute directly or indirectly to the production of travel and tourism services or experiences. There is little value in being able to list all such organisations, although you do need to be aware of the different types of organisations involved and, more importantly, their degree of power or influence within the overall tourism production system. There are different categories of businesses or organisations within the travel and tourism industry/production system:

1 *Principals:* transport operators, accommodation/hospitality providers, attractions, etc.

2 *Intermediaries:* tour operators, travel agencies.

3 *Private sector support:* commercial businesses that directly/ indirectly support travel and tourism.

4 *Public sector support:* governmental and semi-governmental bodies that directly/indirectly support travel and tourism.

5 *Sectoral organisations:* trade and professional bodies representing particular industries/sectors.

6 *Tourism organisations:* private/public bodies with an interest in travel and tourism as a whole.

7 *Destination organisations:* public/private/partnership bodies involved in destination development and/or marketing.

Figure 2.2 provides a simple summary of the structure of the travel and tourism industry.

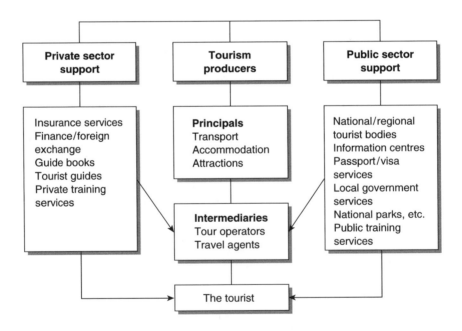

Figure 2.2 The travel and tourism industry

How are the sectors related?

Although the travel and tourism industry is, as we have already seen, diverse and fragmented, relationships do exist between many organisations, particularly those involved in the direct 'production' of tourism. This relationship occurs within the travel and tourism **chain of distribution**, representing in theory a simple link from producers/**principals**, through **intermediaries** (tour operators and retail outlets) to the customer. In reality, the picture is rather more complex. Most principals have their own chain of distribution linking either to retail outlets or direct to the customer (via their own websites or through a **GDS**), while tour operators often 'miss-out' the retail section of the chain through direct sale. **Vertical** and **horizontal integration** in the industry has also resulted in many elements of the chain of distribution, at least within the context of package tourism, being owned by the same organisation. This, in turn, has increased the degree of control enjoyed by major tour operators both over the production of tourism and within the overall tourism system.

Conversely, the rapid growth in online sales (**e.tailing**) has not only further complicated the chain of distribution but also served to limit the power of intermediaries. Many online businesses (dot.coms), such as expedia.com or lastminute.com, sell a variety of travel and tourism products (allowing customers to create their own package holiday), while principals themselves, such as budget airlines, also offer links on their websites to other products, such as accommodation, car hire, insurance and entertainment.

What is the 'product' of the travel and tourism industry?

Most industries are defined by the products they produce. What, however, is the tourism product? There are two related ways of considering this question:

1 *The 'total' tourism product.* The concept of a **total tourism product** was first proposed by Victor Middleton, an academic and tourism consultant who has written extensively on marketing in travel and tourism. The main point is that the tourism product is a collection of tangible and intangible components, including both the products of the industry, such as accommodation, transport and entertainment, but also things such as accessibility, weather, value for money, contacts with local people and the extent

to which expectations are realised. It is important, therefore, to think about the extent to which the travel and tourism industry can influence a tourist's overall enjoyment of a holiday.

A useful way of conceptualising the tourism product is to think of it as the total experience enjoyed (or not, as the case may be!) by tourists from the time they leave home to when they arrive back at home again. Try relating your own tourism/holiday experiences to this, particularly the factors that most pleased or disappointed you.

2 **Tourists as both consumers and producers.** Travel and tourism is a **service industry** (see Section 12 on marketing travel and tourism). Common to all service industries is the concept of **inseparability** (sometimes referred to as simultaneity), or the fact that you cannot separate the production and consumption of a service. Services produced and consumed simultaneously and, therefore, what the travel and tourism industry provides is an interim output, or the potential for services to occur.

Together, these two themes reflect one of the most important points in the study of travel and tourism – that *the tourism 'product' is, in fact, a tourism experience.*

Taking it **FURTHER**

As a means of providing a framework for more detailed analyses of its constituent sectors, the travel and tourism industry is generally studied from two perspectives. First, it is viewed descriptively in terms of its size, scope and characteristics, the emphasis being on its diversity. Second, the inherent power relationships within the industry are often explored and analysed, with particular attention being paid to the alleged dominance of intermediaries/tour operators within the industry. However, there is evidence to suggest that in recent years, and largely as a result of advances in information technology, there has been a shift in the balance of power away from intermediaries towards other elements of the chain of distribution. Both principals and customers are now in a much more powerful position and it is logical, therefore, to consider for how long there will be an identifiable chain of distribution in travel and tourism.

Examiners will assume that you have at least a reasonable grasp of the structure and characteristics of the travel and tourism industry and are likely to be more interested in the extent to which you can use or interpret that knowledge. Therefore, exam questions will usually require you to apply your knowledge of the industry (both conceptual and, as in most areas of travel and tourism, practical) to particular issues.

Within the context of the tourism system, tourism planning and sustainable tourism development, a typical question may be:

"What are the implications of the structure of the travel and tourism industry for the effective management and development of tourism?"

In answering this question, the key issue is the diversity/fragmentation of the industry and the fact that it is, effectively, impossible to control. National/global tourism organisations have, by and large, relatively little control over the industry which itself is increasingly dominated by large, international businesses. Therefore, effective planning and management of tourism at the destination level may require planning restrictions and legislation, though this may be difficult to implement in an era of globalisation and market-led economies.

Alternatively, questions may have a more conceptual focus, such as:

"Industries are defined by their products. What are the products of the travel and tourism industry?"

Two themes are inherent in this question: the nature of travel and tourism products and the travel and tourism 'industry' debate. An answer would ideally start by reviewing the argument that the travel and tourism industry is best seen as a production system, followed by the key point that what it produces are interim outputs (potential services) which become tourist experiences at the point of consumption. The infinitely variable nature of such experiences reinforces the argument that the travel and tourism sector should not be thought of as an industry in the traditional sense of the word.

Textbook guide

HOLLOWAY **(2002):** *Chapter 6*
MILL AND MORRISON **(1998):** *Chapter 1*

6	
transport for travel and tourism	

Transport and tourism are synonymous. Tourism is about travelling to, visiting and experiencing other places and, therefore, transport is an indispensable element of the tourism system, carrying tourists between the generating region and the destination region. Moreover, an important relationship exists between transport and the destination. That is, many destinations have evolved as a result of existing transport networks both to and around the destinations, or have developed as a result of the introduction of transport services. Therefore, an understanding of transport is an essential part of the study of travel and tourism.

Most commonly, perhaps, transport for travel and tourism is associated with air travel. As noted in Section 1, the development of commercial air services has been a major influence on the rapid and continuing growth in international tourism. However, ground travel by car or train remains the most widely used form of tourism transport while a variety of other modes of transport are available. Nevertheless, air transport is one of the most important sectors in terms of international tourism and is dealt with separately in Section 7 of this Companion.

When thinking about transport for tourism, it's important to be able to identify all types of transport both to and at the destination. All transport, whether an international flight, a taxi ride from the airport to the hotel, or hiring a bicycle for a day, is part of the tourism system and, equally, part of the tourist experience.

Typically, the study of transport for tourism focuses on different types of transport. However, you also need to be aware of a number of issues relating to transportation in general, including the relevance of transport to travel and tourism, the component parts of transport networks, and external factors that influence the development of transport. Therefore, the first part of this section highlights these issues before looking at different modes of transport.

The relevance of transport

Virtually all tourism (domestic or international) involves experiencing locations. Therefore, transport facilities, either private or public, are an essential element of travel and tourism. Beyond this rather obvious fact, transport is also relevant because:

- It underpins the development of destinations and other facilities – just as sea-side resorts originally evolved because of the development of railways/railway stations, many contemporary resorts owe their existence to air routes. Similarly, motels were first developed in the USA at major road intersections.
- It is a product of the travel and tourism industry – travel agencies sell a variety of travel services.
- Different modes of transport are often combined within, and contribute to, the overall tourist experience. In some instances (for example, cruising or long-distance rail journeys) transport *is* the experience.

> When considering the contribution of transport to the development of tourism, key factors are the availability of cheap, comfortable and safe forms of mass travel. However, another significant factor is time – popular destinations are easy to get to and, as air travel in particular has developed, the more distant, exotic locations have become more accessible in terms of journey times, and so the pleasure periphery has spread. Conversely, those destinations that take longer to reach (though not necessarily the most distant) tend to retain their exclusivity.

Elements of transport systems

Whatever the mode of transport, all transport systems are made up of a number of elements. These contribute in different ways to different systems but, importantly, they are interconnected and, therefore, the performance of the system is dependent upon each element. These elements are:

1   *The way.* This can be natural and 'free' (air, sea) or constructed (road, rail, canals). The nature of the way is related to flexibility, congestion and so on (though air travel is subject to a variety of regulations).

2   *The vehicle.* This is the actual unit on which people travel, such as trains, ships or aircraft. Related to this is the idea of

'motive power' (except in the case of bicycle travel!) that determines speed and cost of travel, but also has implications in terms of (running theme) sustainable development.

3 *The terminal.* This provides access to the vehicle and, commonly, acts as an interchange between modes of transport. Sometimes, the terminal is the potentially weakest element of the system, as in the limited capacity of many major airports.

4 *Control and communication systems.* All modes of transport are more or less subject to control, such as air traffic control or railway signalling. Road travel is also, of course, subject to control (speed limits, traffic lights, and so on). The purpose of control systems is both efficiency and safety. Communication systems also facilitate transport, whether simple information screens at terminals or sophisticated in-car satellite directional systems.

5 *Management and staff.* The efficient operation of most transport systems is dependent upon an enormous variety of roles, from senior management to more direct service roles, such as check-in at an airport.

When considering the interdependence of these elements, think of examples that demonstrate how a journey can be improved or disrupted by any one element. Traffic jams (the way) interrupt road travel, while signal failure (control) is a frequent source of delay in rail travel. There are also frequent examples of how staff action (strikes) within just one section of an organisation, such as an airline's ground-staff, can paralyse its total operation.

External factors influencing transport

Transport systems cannot operate in isolation from the external political economy; that is, most systems are subject to a variety of factors that may influence their operation and future development. Three key issues to be aware of are:

1 *Regulations and political influences.* Air transport, for example, has traditionally been highly regulated, though deregulation has been a feature of the sector in recent decades (see Section 7).

2 **Competition.** In many parts of the world, transport operators are facing increasing competition from both within their sector and from other modes of transport. For example, cross-Channel ferries, the traditional means of travelling from the UK to mainland Europe, now compete with railways and low-cost airlines.

3 **Environmental concerns.** By its very nature, transport (other than bicycle transport and powered modes that are less dependent on fossil fuels) impacts on the environment.

Modes of transport

There are different modes of transport available to tourists, the choice of which depends upon a variety of factors, including:

- safety
- time/speed
- convenience
- flexibility
- cost
- comfort
- reliability
- availability.

This list is by no means comprehensive as other influences may determine the choice of transport. Tourists may choose a particular mode for the experience it offers or the status it represents – a trip on the Orient Express, or a cycling holiday, or prior to its decommissioning, a flight on Concorde are obvious examples. Conversely, there may be no realistic alternative choice. Nevertheless, these factors present a useful basis for examining different modes of transport and, from a tourist's point of view, the benefits and disadvantages of each.

For the purposes of most travel and tourism courses, you do not need to have a detailed knowledge of the structure, operations and management of different modes of transport (although air transport is a possible exception). It is more important to understand the relationship between particular modes of transport, the benefits they offer and the travel and tourism experience.

Road transport

Overall, travel by road is the most popular mode of transport, though it tends to be limited to relatively shorter journeys. Road transport is subdivided into a number of categories:

- Private car: the most ubiquitous mode of transport that offers significant benefits.
- Car rental: a popular transport 'add-on' while at the destination.
- Taxi: a compromise between car hire and public transport.
- Bus/coach: tourists can use either scheduled services or organised tours.
- Cycling: though cycle ways do not always follow roads (old railway routes, for example, are often converted into cycle ways), cycle tourism is, essentially, a form of road transport which has grown in popularity as well as gaining increased attention among tourism academics.

Rail transport

Although the development of the railways heralded the evolution of modern, mass tourism, rail travel's share of contemporary holiday/ tourist travel is relatively small. Moreover, particularly within Europe, it is now losing out to low-cost air travel. Nevertheless, rail travel offers a number of benefits in terms of safety, comfort, reliability and point-to-point (city centre) transport while, for tourists, rail travel can offer a number of experiences:

- Longer rail journeys: trips that are taken as a holiday/travel experience, such as the Trans-Siberian railway or rail journeys through the Canadian Rockies.
- 'Authentic' travel (running theme): for example, journeys on steam trains.
- Guided tours by train: a number of tour operators offer rail-based tours, such as India by rail.
- 'Little railways': short, narrow-gauge railway lines.

Water-borne transport

Transport on water (sea or inland waterways) is a popular mode of tourist travel and is explored in some detail in Holloway's *The Business of Tourism*. Water-borne transport is available in a variety of forms, although a useful means of categorising is to distinguish between water-borne transport as a journey and as a tourist/holiday experience:

1 **Water-borne journeys.** These are trips on water between two points, the most popular form being ferry trips. In some cases, ocean liners may fall into this category (that is, for those who choose it in preference to, say, flying between two points). Ferries may be large ships that carry cars and provide overnight accommodation, or smaller crafts, including hovercraft and hydro-foils, for shorter journeys.

2 *Water-borne tourist experiences.* Cruising, once the preserve of the wealthy, has become increasingly popular. It tends to be geographically defined, the Mediterranean, the Caribbean and the South pacific being popular routes, although cruises now embrace more distant regions, such as the Southern Ocean or the Arctic. Other water-borne experiences include yachting flotilla holidays and, on inland waters, river and canal cruising.

Taking it *FURTHER*

Transport is an essential element of travel and tourism. Therefore, continued growth in tourism will depend on the increasing use of existing transport facilities, the provision of new facilities, or a combination of the two. However, while the growth of travel and tourism is associated with economic and other benefits to destinations, attention has been increasingly paid to the environmental costs of transport. That is, virtually all powered transport has an environmental impact in terms of pollution and use of non-renewable resources (oil) and, as a result, the issue of transport has become more significant within the context of sustainable tourism development. How, then, can transport for tourism be more environmentally sustainable? By encouraging alternative modes of transport? By imposing an 'eco-tax' on aviation fuel? Or even, perhaps, influencing tourism demand?

There are two ways of studying transport for travel and tourism: from the perspective of different modes of transport or from an overall perspective of transport as an element of the tourism system. Consequently, exam questions may also be influenced by either perspective, though the kind of questions you are likely to be asked will be obvious to you from the way that the subject has been approached in your lectures and from the particular interest of your lecturer. If he or she has a background in transport, then you are more likely to be set 'technical' questions relating to a specific mode of transport.

From a broader, travel and tourism perspective, questions will certainly focus on transport within the context of the tourism system. For example:

" Critically evaluate the interdependence of the elements of travel systems to the tourist experience. "

All travel systems depend on the efficient interaction and contribution of the different elements of the system. Your answer should identify and explain these elements, and consider the relative importance of each within differing contexts. Further depth of analysis could then be provided by considering the pressures on each element as the demand for tourism continues to increase, and the likely challenges for transport operators.

The environmental impact of transport is an important issue. Commonly, questions relate to the 'problem' of the motor car. For example:

" How successful are policies to reduce our dependency on the car likely to be, and what would be their impact on travel and tourism? "

The private car remains the most flexible mode of transport and, for both domestic and international tourism (where cross-border travel is relatively easy, as within Europe, for example), it is likely to remain the most popular form of travel. A variety of policies have been proposed to reduce this dependency which, if successful, would impact on travel and tourism in a number of ways, but particularly reducing the demand for destinations or types of tourism that are car-dependent.

Finally, questions may relate transport to tourism demand. You might be asked to:

" Consider how changes in the demand for tourism will impact upon the transport sector. "

Highlighting trends and changes in tourism demand, such as the growth in independent travel, the alleged emergence of the new tourist, the increasing demand for more adventurous forms of tourism in more distant, exotic destinations, and so on, your answer should explore the implications for different modes of transport in terms of routes, ease of access, quality and experience. At the same time, however, you should also note that although the transport sector must be responsive to changes in tourism demand, developments in transport can also influence that demand.

Textbook guide

COOPER ET AL. (2005): *Chapter 13*
HOLLOWAY (2002): *Chapters 8 and 9*
PAGE (1999)
SHARPLEY (2002): *Chapter 7*

7
air transport

As noted in the previous section, transport is synonymous with travel and tourism. To be able to participate in tourism, people must travel; to travel, people must, generally, have access to some form of transport. Therefore, the evolution of various modes of transport has been integral to the growth of tourism in general, while the development of air transport in particular has been of fundamental importance to the growth of international mass tourism. In other words, reliable, cheap, fast and convenient public transport is a prerequisite for mass market travel and, over the last half-century, this need has been met in the international context by developments within the airline sector.

> *The airline industry itself is a fascinating subject of study. That is, the historical and technological development of the industry, the business of airline operations, the emergence of the 'no-frills' budget airlines and the dramatic challenges faced by the world's major international carriers in the early years of the 21st century are all interesting topics in their own right. However, always try to look beyond these specific issues to consider how changes and developments within the airline industry have influenced or impacted on the development of travel and tourism.*

As with many areas of travel and tourism, air transport is a broad, dynamic and fascinating subject. Nevertheless, few travel and tourism texts deal with it exclusively – it is usually referred to either in chapters on transport in introductory tourism texts or along with other modes of transport in texts devoted to transport for tourism. However, it is well worth looking at specialist books on the subject, particularly to support your assignment work or exam revision. One key writer on the subject is Rigas Doganis, who is the author of a number of widely read books on air transport.

Bearing in mind that what we are interested in is the relationship between air transport and the development of travel and tourism, there are five key (and related) themes that you should become familiar with. These are:

- The historical/technological development of the airline sector and its importance to the development of tourism.
- Regulation, deregulation (liberalisation) and privatisation in the air industry.
- Airline operations: schedules, charter and no-frill/low-cost airlines.
- The relationship between air transport and airports.
- Strategic alliances in the airline industry.

The development of the airline sector

While the development of air transport has, without a doubt, been the most significant and influential factor in the growth and development of international mass tourism, it is important to understand why and how this is so. With respect to the 'why', there are two principal factors to be aware of:

1 *Technological advances.* Since the 1950s, rapid advances in aircraft design and engine technology have made air travel faster, safer, more comfortable and, most importantly, cheaper. The key factor has been the continual reduction in the seat cost per passenger in both absolute terms and also relative to other forms of transport, resulting from both aircraft design (the introduction of the wide-bodied jet, or 'jumbo' in 1970, being of particular significance) and engine technology, with more efficient engines further reducing costs. The planned introduction of the Airbus 380 'super-jumbo' by 2007 is an example of continuing technological advance, though it remains to be seen how many airlines buy this new aircraft. The development of **short take-off and landing (STOL)** aircraft has also been important to business travel.

2 *Business strategies.* As the airline industry has become increasingly competitive, largely as a result of **deregulation** or **liberalisation**, airlines have looked for ways of attracting more passengers. These have included various fare-reduction schemes or frequent flyer programmes, but the most significant development in recent years (resulting from technology-induced cost reductions) has been the introduction of low-cost/no-frills operations, initially in the United States but now within Europe and elsewhere. The era of **strategic alliances** within air transport has also served to make air services both cheaper and more convenient, hence more attractive, while charter airlines have, over the last thirty years, been fundamental to the success of mass package tourism.

Regarding *how* these developments in air transport have directly influenced travel and tourism, a number of points are of relevance:

- A clear relationship exists in general between the growth in air transport passenger numbers and the growth in international tourism.
- The competitive strategy of airlines has a direct influence on the geography on tourism. Within Europe, for example, north–south flows have been dictated to a great extent by charter flights, while low-cost carriers are fundamentally changing patterns of intra-European tourist travel.
- Some destinations have been 'created' by air transport (that is, to where other viable means of transport are not available).
- Increasing efficiencies have brought more distant destinations within the reach of mass tourism.

The most dramatic change in short-haul air travel in recent years has been brought about by the rise of the low-cost carriers. It is well worth considering the wider implications of this on tourism demand and flows, as well as associated impacts such as regional airport development, international second home ownership, and so on.

Regulation, deregulation (liberalisation) and privatisation

Underpinning many of the transformations in, and challenges facing, the airline industry has been the process of deregulation (US) or liberalisation (Europe) of airline operations. While some regulation remains necessary (safety, maintenance, traffic control, operating licences, and so on), deregulation/liberalisation refers to the removal of restrictive or protectionist policies with regards to the business of airline operations. While you need to focus on the implications of deregulation/liberalisation for travel and tourism, an awareness of the process leading up to the development of open-skies policies is also necessary. Points to be familiar with include:

- the benefits/disadvantages of regulation
- bi-lateral agreements and the **five freedoms** of the air
- US deregulation policies and outcomes
- the EU liberalisation packages and outcomes.

Key to understanding deregulation is the fact that its purpose is to create greater competition within the airline industry by, for example, open access to all routes, no restrictions on new entrants to the market, the right of airlines to set their own fares, no restrictions on capacity or frequency and, within Europe, **cabotage** rights and a move towards privatising previously state-owned national carriers. This has, to an extent, occurred and, consequently, air passengers have greater choice in terms of price, routes, and so on. However, it has also led to the emergence of mega-carriers, the collapse of many airlines and, potentially, greater concentration of ownership within the sector.

It is well worth exploring the changing structure of the international airline industry that has resulted from deregulation.

Airline operations

There are, essentially, three types of airline operation. Each has advantages and disadvantages for both the operator and the customer:

1 *Scheduled flights:* operate on defined routes, usually from and to major airports, for which they have been licensed. They must operate according to timetables, irrespective of demand. In order to reduce the inevitable higher costs, many airlines have developed **hub-and-spoke systems** to achieve greater efficiencies.

2 *Charter flights:* freedom to cancel/change departures; work on higher **load factors** with lower levels of service, off-peak flying, etc. For tourists, charter flights provide cheap transport to holiday destinations although levels of comfort and service are low.

3 *Low-cost/no frills flights:* often from and to regional airports, minimal levels of service, fast turnrounds, high load factors, distribution via the Internet, etc. The basis of their efficiency restricts the distance over which they may operate. For passengers, the principal benefit is the low cost.

Air transport and airports

As noted in the previous section, one of the elements on which an efficient transport system depends is the terminal: in the case of air transport, the airport. One of the greatest challenges facing the future development of air transport is the lack of airport capacity in terms of both aircraft movements and passenger volumes. This has implications for the future development of tourism and, although some countries have developed new airports to maintain their growth in tourist arrivals (for example, Hong Kong), many international airports in Europe and the USA are operating at capacity. A number of airports are developing their terminals in anticipation of the new super-jumbo, although additional runway capacity remains a pressing issue (with significant environmental consequences) for most major international airports.

> Most major international airports, particularly in Europe and the USA, are operating at capacity. For many, the answer is seen to lie in the building of new runways and the design of new terminal buildings that are more efficient at handling large numbers of passengers. However, it is also important to consider the accessibility of airports themselves. In the UK, for example, regional airports are becoming increasingly popular as they are more accessible and user-friendly.

Strategic alliances in the airline industry

A particular feature of the international airline industry in recent years has been the development of alliances. In order to overcome many of the constraints imposed by the regulation of international air operations, many airlines have developed globally-based alliance networks that offer alliance members a number of competitive advantages, including:

- complementary route networks
- access to other countries/continents
- runway slots/terminal gates at congested airports
- domestic feeder services
- economies through shared services (maintenance, etc.).

There are four major international alliances: the Star Alliance, the One World Alliance, the Sky Team Alliance and the Wings Alliance. Collectively, these represent the increasing globalisation of the international airline industry.

Taking it **FURTHER**

The relationship between air transport and the development of travel and tourism is widely recognised. Not only are tourist flows, in many instances, largely determined by air transport, but many destinations owe their very existence to air transport. Moreover, ongoing developments in the airline industry, primarily resulting from deregulation, continue to influence the nature of travel and tourism. However, airlines face a challenging future and a number of questions should be addressed. For example, as continuing growth in air travel is forecast, does the capacity exist to handle such growth, particularly airport capacity? Is there likely to be a move towards global open-skies as the competitive benefits of deregulation are more widely recognised? And, perhaps most importantly, as airlines increasingly face low levels of profitability, are economic efficiencies likely to be sought or will air travel become more expensive?

There are a variety of different questions that you may be asked relating to air transport, focusing on issues such as advances in aircraft design and technology (for example, the development of the super-jumbo), the deregulation debate, strategic alliances within the airline industry, the emergence and growth of no-frills airlines, or the challenges of airport capacity. For most questions relating to the subject, some knowledge or understanding of the process and implications of deregulation should be seen as essential – you will find that you will need to refer directly or indirectly to this issue to support your answers.

With respect to the dramatic growth of low-cost/no-frills carriers, you may be asked:

"What future influence will low-cost carriers have on domestic and international tourist flows?"

The emergence of low-cost carriers has had a dramatic impact on tourist flows both nationally and internationally. Exploring the ways in which low-cost carriers operate and the regulatory environment which has encouraged their growth, your answer should review their impact on regional airport development, on the growth of new destinations, on the demand for tourism and on alternative modes of transport. Future impacts should also be considered within the context of the factors that enable low-cost airline operations.

A particular feature of international air transport has been the development of alliances. Typically, you will be asked to consider the benefits and costs of airline alliances:

"What are the pros and cons of airline alliances and how likely are we to see more alliances in the future?"

Referring to existing alliances, answers should consider the reasons why (and how) airlines develop alliances and the commercial/competitive advantages they provide, as well as the potential benefits to passengers. At the same time, the potential for anti-competitive behaviour and the long-term domination of international air transport by a small number of powerful alliances may represent a future threat to a competitive market, with implications for passenger choice and the cost of air travel.

As further economies are sought through technological innovation in aircraft design, two strategies are emerging: on the one hand, the development of larger, super-jumbos and, on the other hand, more efficient, smaller aircraft capable of flying longer distances. In this context, you may be asked to:

"Critically assess the potential influence of the new super-jumbo aircraft on travel and tourism."

While the new generation of super-jumbos will offer the opportunity for significant economies of scale, such benefits might be limited by the fact that, in terms of operations, routes and destinations will be restricted by the ability (or desire) of airports to accommodate the new aircraft. Major airports will have to make significant investment in new terminals, while airlines may have to develop more effective hub-and-spoke systems or alliances to obtain appropriate load factors. Moreover, as air passengers demand more flexibility, point-to-point flights on smaller aircraft, often avoiding over-congested major airports, may be more appealing.

Textbook guide

COOPER ET AL. (2005): *Chapter 13*
DOGANIS (2004)
HOLLOWAY (2002): *Chapter 7*
LUMSDEN AND PAGE (2004)
PENDER AND SHARPLEY (2005): *Chapter 3*
SHARPLEY (2002): *Chapter 7*

8	
accommodation	

The accommodation sector is the largest sector of the tourism industry. It is also the most important; not only do most tourists require overnight accommodation during their journey or stay in the destination, but it also frequently represents the most significant element of total tourism expenditure. Therefore, the accommodation sector is a fundamental part of the tourism economy and also a vital ingredient of the tourism experience.

In practice, the accommodation sector is one of the most dynamic elements of the travel and tourism industry. It is well worth familiarising yourself with the major hotel organisations (domestic and international) and keeping up to date with changes and developments in the industry. An easy way to do this is to register (free of charge) with relevant online organisations, such as travelmole.com, ehotelier.com or wiredhotelier.com.

Although the accommodation sector is also just one part of the **hospitality industry**, for our purposes it can be studied from three perspectives. The emphasis placed on each may vary – on some courses, for example, accommodation is looked at only briefly in the context of the structure of the tourism industry whereas, on other courses, an entire unit/module might be devoted to the subject. Nevertheless, some understanding of accommodation from all three perspectives will undoubtedly help you in your assignments and exams.

Accommodation within the tourism system

From the tourism system perspective, the accommodation sector is most frequently assessed descriptively in terms of its scope and scale. In other words, many textbooks focus on defining the accommodation sector, highlighting the enormous variety of types of accommodation. A useful way of doing this is to categorise accommodation under four different headings:

1 Commercial (i.e. for profit): *serviced*

2 Commercial: *non-serviced*

3 Non-commercial (i.e. not-for-profit): *serviced*

4 Non-commercial: *non-serviced.*

An alternative means of categorising accommodation is by markets. The main distinction is between the business and leisure markets, which will often define both the location of accommodation and the services provided. Similarly, hotels may be categorised by location – resort-based hotels, city centre hotels, airport hotels and rural hotels, for example, attract different markets and face different challenges related to their locations. However, it is also important to note the relative importance of the domestic and international markets to different accommodation providers.

> *It is also important to remember that accommodation can also be cross-sectoral. That is, it does not exist in isolation from, but is directly related to other sectors of the travel and tourism industry, as in the case of cruise ships, long-distance rail journeys (for example, Trans-Siberian railway) or all-inclusive resorts.*

More relevant than simple definition or description, however, is the relationship between the accommodation sector and the tourism industry/system as a whole – hence, the study of accommodation is synonymous with the running themes of the tourism industry and the tourism system. The accommodation sector both influences, and is influenced by, other elements of the tourism system as well as certain factors external to the system. In particular, you should be familiar with the influence of:

- the development of travel and tourism, in particular transport networks and tour operations, on accommodation development
- the nature of tourism demand on accommodation development and operation
- the nature and scale of accommodation on destination development
- the nature and scale of accommodation on tourism demand
- the centrality of accommodation to the tourist experience
- external forces (economic, political, etc.) on the success of the accommodation sector.

The national/international hotel industry

While it is important to consider accommodation within the broader context of the tourism system, you should also have some understanding of the accommodation sector as an industry in its own right. There are two levels at which the industry can be assessed, namely, from the macro perspective (the industry as a whole) and the micro perspective (managing hotel operations). Despite the enormous variety of types of accommodation, attention is paid primarily to the commercial hotel sector, this being the most significant in business terms.

A fundamental characteristic of the hotel industry is the distinction between **independent hotels** and **chain hotels**; the former being more common, for historical reasons, in Europe, the latter more dominant elsewhere. Therefore, an important theme is the structure of the hotel industry, both domestically and internationally, in terms of ownership and the resultant characteristics of supply. Whereas independent hotels may be associated with individuality, chain hotels imply greater standardisation, potentially contributing to the (running theme) process of globalisation. It is important to note that, from the 'league tables' of major international hotel chains, the global supply of accommodation remains largely dominated by American and European businesses.

> *Try to remember that, whether independent or chain, the objectives of commercial hotel operations are to optimise returns (i.e. to maximise profit!). Frequently, hotels and/or hotel chains are owned by large corporations or investment companies and, therefore, their structure and strategies are driven by the need to make a return on stakeholders' investment.*

The structure or ownership of hotel chains is more complex than might be imagined. For example, just because a hotel is called a Marriott does not necessarily mean it is owned (or even managed) by the Marriott organisation. Two issues are, therefore, important to consider – models of ownership/operation and branding.

Models of ownership/operation

An important distinction exists between the ownership and management of a hotel. A hotel chain does not necessarily own all, or even any, of its properties and, commonly, larger hotel chains are characterised by a combination of ownership or operational structures. These may also reflect the corporate strategy adopted by the organisation (see Section 13). Typically, hotel chains may adopt one or more of the following:

- *Owner/operator of hotels*: this is related to growth by acquisition.
- *Franchising*: where the hotel is owned and operated by a franchise partner.
- *Management contracting:* where the hotel company manages a hotel on behalf of the owners.

You should familiarise yourself with the advantages and disadvantages of each model of ownership and operation, and to be able to relate these to the actual strategies of international hotel chains. A particularly good case study is the Accor group, although most of the larger chains employ a combination of ownership and operational structures.

Independent hotels often become members of a **hotel consortium** in order to compete more effectively with chains while retaining the advantages of independent operation and the individuality of their products and service.

Branding

Related to ownership and operational structures, branding has become an increasingly important strategic tool for hotel groups. As a form of **market segmentation**, it is a process whereby hotel companies develop recognisable brands to meet the needs of particular markets, usually based on price and levels of service. A current trend is towards the development of budget hotel brands, such as Formule 1, Campanile and Travelodge.

Accommodation operations

To an extent, all forms of accommodation face similar management challenges and issues, although the significance of each will vary according to the nature of the accommodation. Unless you are taking a joint tourism–hospitality course or undertaking a detailed assignment in hotel operations you would not normally be required to know about these in detail. However, you should be aware of these issues, their potential significance and their interdependence.

Economic issues

The accommodation sector tends to have high fixed costs relative to variable costs. Therefore, hotels need to achieve **occupancy levels** to meet both those fixed costs and the variable costs that increase as occupancy increases, although extra income may be earned through the provision of ancillary services. The setting of **room rates** and **yield management** are two factors that can determine occupancy and profitability.

Demand issues

Related to occupancy levels, the demand for accommodation is influenced by the location of the premises, the fixity of premises and **seasonality/periodicity**.

Quality issues

Quality is important from two perspectives. First, **classification** and **grading** schemes are useful marketing tools, the former indicating the range of products/services available and the latter indicating their overall quality. Second, as customers become more quality and value conscious, service quality management is playing an increasingly important role.

Technology issues

As with most sectors of the travel and tourism industry, technological advances are having a significant impact on operations. Within the accommodation sector, yield management systems have contributed to occupancy and profitability, while GDS and Internet booking have had a positive impact on demand.

Environmental issues

The accommodation sector has become more aware of environmental issues for both efficiency and ethical reasons. The International Hotels Environment Initiative is a good example of a sector-wide programme.

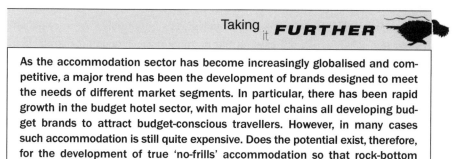

Taking it **FURTHER**

As the accommodation sector has become increasingly globalised and competitive, a major trend has been the development of brands designed to meet the needs of different market segments. In particular, there has been rapid growth in the budget hotel sector, with major hotel chains all developing budget brands to attract budget-conscious travellers. However, in many cases such accommodation is still quite expensive. Does the potential exist, therefore, for the development of true 'no-frills' accommodation so that rock-bottom prices can be charged?

The type of questions you are likely to be asked will, of course, vary according to the depth in which the subject of accommodation is covered on your course, although they are most likely to focus on overall trends. For example, the most noticeable trend in recent years has been the development of the budget hotel sector, and so you may be asked:

❝What are implications of the growth in the supply of budget hotels for the accommodation sector as a whole?❞

Budget hotels have become increasingly widespread and popular in recent years, meeting the needs of budget-conscious travellers who do not require a range of services. Their attraction, of course, lies in their price, although there are disadvantages related to location, the lack of services and so on. Nevertheless, non-budget hotels/chains will need to develop more targeted brands and to promote their benefits to specific markets in order to compete, as well as developing their own budget brands.

Conversely, you may be asked about the thorny issue of grading hotels:

" Given the diversity of the international hotel sector, how meaningful are grading and classification schemes? "

A variety of grading and classification schemes exist nationally and internationally, while many tour operators and other travel organisations also attach their own grading schemes to hotels. To an extent, such schemes reflect the quality of an establishment yet perceptions of quality vary enormously. As a minimum, recognised schemes should exist at the national level although for larger hotel chains, the development of internationally recognised brands represents a better measure of quality.

Textbook guide

COOPER ET AL. (2005): *Chapter 11*
HOLLOWAY (2002): *Chapter 10*
SHARPLEY (2002): *Chapter 8*

9	
attractions	

Attractions, often referred to as either tourist attractions or visitor attractions, are a fundamental element of the travel and tourism system. In a sense, they 'make' the destination – an attraction, literally, attracts tourists to a place, providing them with a reason to visit or stay there. Therefore, attractions are a catalyst for travel and tourism, creating opportunities for the development of transport, accommodation, tours/guides, souvenir production, and so on. In short, many travel and tourism destinations owe their place on the domestic or international tourism map (and their local tourism industry) to the existence of one or more attractions.

A useful and interesting exercise that emphasises the importance of attractions to the tourism system is to compile a list of well-known destinations that have developed as a result of one or more attractions – or, indeed, of major attractions that are, perhaps, better known than the places where they are located!

There is, of course, an almost infinite variety of attractions in terms of type and purpose. In some cases, the entire destination might be an attraction (for example, the English Lake District) while, in other cases, attractions might serve a number of purposes other than tourism – religious buildings, art galleries and museums for example, fall into this category. Moreover, from an academic perspective, attention is often paid to sub-themes, such as the management of **heritage attractions** or even so-called '**dark tourism**', while the subject of visitor management (see Section 19) is frequently considered under the umbrella of attractions or attractions management. At the same time, the running theme of authenticity (and Dean MacCannell's concept of **staged authenticity**) is highly relevant to the study of attractions. It is, therefore, a broad topic that interconnects with other areas of travel and tourism, though the textbook guide below lists books that cover the subject in some depth.

As with many other areas of travel and tourism, the study of attractions 'comes to life' if you can relate theories or concepts to specific real-world examples. Indeed, examiners will expect you to be able to refer to a variety of examples in assignments or exam questions on the subject. Therefore, you should 'collect' a number of relevant case studies of different attractions that you can refer to.

Given its breadth and complexity, most units or modules adopt an approach that takes an overview of the attractions component of the tourism system, typically considering four principal themes. These provide the basis for considering different types of attractions, different settings or different developmental purposes in more detail.

The importance of the attraction

As already noted, the importance of attractions to the destination cannot be overemphasised. All destinations require a variety of tourist services and amenities, such as accommodation and catering, as well as the appropriate transport infrastructure to and within the destination. First and foremost, however, for all destinations there is the 'rule of thumb' that tourists must have a reason to visit, a reason to stay and a reason to return.

It is attractions that provide these reasons. Therefore, it is important for destinations to maintain and effectively manage their attractions and, where necessary, develop new ones. The type, scale and number of attractions varies according to the destination; there may be a single **flagship attraction**, such as the Taj Mahal at Agra in India, or destinations may seek to develop a **critical mass** of attractions, as in many major city destinations.

Types of attractions

Not surprisingly, it is difficult, if not impossible, to define attractions, although there are a number of factors that, from a travel and tourism perspective, contribute to an understanding of what an attraction is. An attraction should:

- be permanent (permanently established or regularly repeated)
- be enjoyable, entertaining and/or educational
- attract visitors
- be effectively managed to meet all stakeholders' needs.

> *Perhaps the most important feature of an attraction is that it can be managed in order to optimise the benefits to visitors, to local people and to the destination as a whole. The focus of such management is largely determined by the nature/type/purpose of the attraction.*

A variety of attempts have been made to classify attractions, the purpose being to identify specific issues or challenges that are relevant to different types of attraction. At the simplest level, attractions can be listed by type (for example, craft centres, theme parks, religious attractions, rural attractions, and so on). However, there is often overlap between these types and so it is more useful to classify attractions according to other criteria. Anna Leask's model of classification (Fyall et al., 2003) neatly summarises these, though the typical categories are:

1 *Ownership.*

- Privately owned attractions. The primary purpose is earning a profit for owners/shareholders; the emphasis, therefore, is on effective business development, focusing on marketing and customer satisfaction.
- Publicly owned attractions. Frequently supported by public funding, their original purpose is often, but not always, to provide a service to local communities, though tourists may be the most numerous visitors. The focus tends to be contributing to local quality of life, although commercial operations (retail, refreshments, etc.) may also be a significant activity.

2 *Origins.*

- Natural attractions. Frequently, the main challenge is to manage visitors to maintain the integrity of the attraction.
- Man-made attractions. This can be subdivided into attractions purposefully built for tourists, and those created for purposes other than tourism. The former includes theme parks, holiday centres, and '**edutainment**' centres, while the latter includes religious and historic buildings.

3 *Markets.*

- Attractions may be classified by their actual/potential markets (volume and origin) which will, in turn, determine the management of the attraction with regard to, for example, marketing, facilities and interpretation.

4 *The core experience.*

- All attractions provide some sort of core experience to visitors – education, excitement, fun, physical activity, etc.

Developing attractions

Managing attractions for travel and tourism is not only about managing existing attractions. As destinations seek to remain competitive, or to develop a tourism industry, developing new attractions is also an important function in terms of both the attraction itself and its contribution to broader objectives.

New attractions, particularly flagship attractions which benefit from public financial support, are not only developed to attract tourists, but they are often designed to contribute to local sustainable development, to enhance the image of the area, or to raise confidence among local communities. Therefore, it is well worth considering these broader objectives and how much they influence the location, nature and design of attractions.

In developing a new attraction, there are five developmental stages:

1 *Conceptual stage:* the idea is measured against available resources, likely demand, etc.

2 *Project design:* costings, designs, etc.

3 *Feasibility study:* including research into potential demand, appropriate locations and an environmental audit.

4 *Development of the attraction:* building the attraction and associated infrastructure, provision of additional services such as refreshments and retail.

5 *Managing the customer experience:* the actual operation of the attraction.

Alternatively, key issues to be considered in the development of an attraction are: resources, the nature of the product (particularly its location), its potential markets, and its day-to-day management.

Assessing the nature of the product, its location and potential markets are vital aspects of attraction development. This is evidenced by recent experience in the UK, where a number of major, publicly funded attractions have either under-performed or closed down simply because of low visitor numbers.

Management issues

Key to the success of an attraction, whether existing or new, is effective day-to-day management. Given the almost limitless variety of types of attractions, there is no single approach to their operational management. Nevertheless, you need to be aware of a number of management issues relevant to many, if not all, attractions:

1 *Financial management.* Attractions need to make a profit or, in the case of publicly owned and subsidised attractions, minimise costs. Therefore, pricing and other activities must focus on covering (usually high) fixed and variable costs, and on generating sufficient revenue for marketing and future investment.

2 *Human resource management.* Staff performance is of fundamental importance in the service industry context. There is a need to focus on quality and motivation in an industry that is often low paid and that may depend, to a great extent, on seasonal labour.

3 *Marketing.* There is a need to undertake a variety of marketing functions, including linking the core experience to appropriate markets and maintaining out-of-season tourist flows.

4 *Visitor management.* Visitors must be managed in order to optimise their experience and to minimise their impact on the attraction and the local environment.

Taking it **FURTHER**

There can be no doubting the importance of attractions to travel and tourism in general, and to destinations in particular. In fact, at their core, tourist destinations are simply a collection of attractions – the purpose of other facilities, such as accommodation, catering and transport, is to enable tourists to visit and enjoy the destination's attractions. Therefore, although much of the study of attractions is concerned with defining and classifying attractions and with exploring appropriate management techniques at the level of the individual attraction, there is also a need to consider attractions within the broader context of the destination. Indeed, perhaps the biggest challenge facing the sector is the issue of supply or over-supply, suggesting that the development of attractions should be considered within broader tourism destination and regional development policies.

Questions on attractions and attraction management usually follow one of two themes: the actual management of attractions and the wider role or influence of attractions within the tourism system. Therefore, an exam question may simply ask:

"What makes a successful attraction?"

This can be looked at from both the development process (that is, the necessary stages and processes of developing an attraction) and the ongoing operational management of attractions. You would need to explore the different categories of attraction to both define the meaning of 'success' in the context of different types of attraction and to identify the key management tasks for each.

Relating attractions to the tourism system, you may be asked:

"How is a tourism destination defined by its attractions?"

Focusing on the concept that a destination and its attractions are synonymous and that attractions act as a catalyst for the development of other amenities, facilities and services, this question requires an analysis of different types of attraction and mixes of attractions, and how these influence the image of a destination, the demand for tourism and the supply of other tourist services.

Increasingly, the development of major flagship attractions is seen as an effective means of developing travel and tourism, and tourism destinations although, in some cases, expensive and highly publicised attractions are less successful than might be hoped. Therefore, a typical question might be:

"Critically analyse the role of flagship attractions in the development of travel and tourism."

Drawing on examples of both successful and unsuccessful developments, your answer should define 'flagship' attractions and their potential contribution to stimulating demand and influencing the development of other attractions and facilities in a destination. The relationship with the wider development of the destination/region should also be referred to, pointing to the need for effective planning and management both of the attraction itself and its development within the context of regional development objectives.

Textbook guide

COOPER ET AL. (2005): *Chapter 10*
FYALL, GARROD AND LEASK (2003)
SHARPLEY (2002): *Chapter 9*
SWARBROOKE (2000)

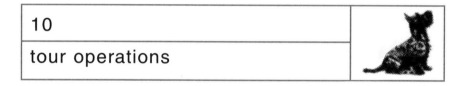

10

tour operations

Tour operators have long played a dominant role in the production and distribution of travel and tourism. In fact, as we saw in Section 1, the emergence of a sophisticated and innovative travel industry was a key factor in the growth and development of international mass tourism, with the tour operating sector in particular leading the way in both creating and meeting the needs of tourists. More recently, of course, a variety of factors, including the increasing supply of 'no-frills' flights, advances in information technology, widespread use of the Internet, and a more confident and experienced travelling public, have all contributed to an increase in independent travel. However, the continuing role and influence of tour operators should not be underestimated, particularly the pivotal position they occupy within the tourism system.

As with many other topics within travel and tourism, the extent to which tour operations are covered will vary from one course to another. In some cases, entire modules are devoted to the subject and you may find yourself being required to create a package holiday as part of your assessment, going through the same process that tour operators follow in practice. Usually, however, you will be expected to understand more generally the role, function, structure and influence of the tour operating sector within the overall travel and tourism industry, as well as having some knowledge of the contemporary practice of tour operating and the challenges faced by tour operators.

> *Surprisingly few texts deal with tour operating in any depth. However, you can learn much about the practice of tour operating by familiarising yourself with the structure of the sector, and the major national and international companies, and by keeping yourself up to date with the activities of major tour operators in terms of their marketing and product development activities. This can be done by regularly reading appropriate trade journals or, as with other aspects of the travel industry, registering with online travel industry news services, such as travelmole.com or eturbonews.com.*

As a starting point, it is essential to understand what tour operations actually are. The best way to do this is to think in terms of what tour operators produce – that is, the package holiday or **inclusive tour**. A package holiday is simply defined as the pre-arranged combination of two or more components of a holiday, such as transport, accommodation and other services (for example, local sightseeing tours). Thus, although package holidays (and, hence, tour operations) are most commonly thought of in terms of charter flights to summer-sun destinations, it is important to recognise the enormous variety of types of package holiday. They can be categorised by:

- *Mode of transport*: package holidays include transport by air (**ITX** or **ITC**), sea, rail, road or car/bicycle hire.
- *Type of accommodation*: any type of accommodation may be component of a package holiday.
- *Services included*: from basic flights and transfer to the '**all-inclusive**'.
- *International vs domestic*: numerous tour operators cater to domestic markets.
- *Distance to destination*: while **short haul** destinations account for the majority of package holidays by air, there is an increasing demand for **long haul** packages.

Package holidays are, therefore, assembled by individuals or organisations (tour operators) that buy products from producers (principals), combine them into a single product (the holiday) and sell them on to the customer. Thus, a key concept is the position of tour operators as **intermediaries** in the chain of distribution. It is through their intermediary position that they are able to fulfil their role by meeting the needs of two groups within the tourism system:

1 *The needs of principals.* The attraction of tour operators to producers/principals lies in their ability to reach a large customer base and in their access to distribution channels to sell their products.

2 *The needs of customers.* Despite the increasing popularity of independent travel booked over the Internet and an increase in so-called **dynamic packaging**, tour operators offer a number of benefits to tourists. These include:

- Low prices: bulk purchasing means that tour operators can often secure significantly lower prices for transport and accommodation.
- Convenience: tour operators are, in a sense, a one-stop shop for a holiday.
- Reliability: the products that operators sell are, in principle, tried and tested.
- Consumer protection: the legal requirement that, at least in Europe, tour operators should be bonded and provide the scope and standards of service that they advertise means that tourists are protected against poor levels of quality/service or, in the extreme, tour operator failure.

However, a term that is increasingly referred to in travel and tourism is **disintermediation**, or the process by which intermediaries in the travel and tourism industry play a declining role in the chain of distribution.

> *It is important to remember that, as intermediaries in the travel and tourism chain of distribution, tour operators not only meet the needs of principals and customers but also are able to exert enormous power over both destinations and tourists by being in the position to dictate the volume and type of tourist flows. This is of particular significance to the concepts (and running themes) of sustainable tourism development and governance.*

The structure of the tour operating sector

Typically, the tour operating sector comprises of a large number of small tour operators but is dominated by a small number of large, international organisations – this is certainly the case throughout Europe and in North America. Therefore, the running theme of globalisation is relevant to the study of tour operations. However, while it is both interesting and useful to explore the actual structure of the sector (most textbooks provide charts detailing 'who owns what'), it is more important for you to appreciate the processes which have brought about its contemporary structure.

Generally, in recent years the tour operating sector has undergone a process of integration or concentration. Such integration has occurred in two directions:

1 **Horizontal integration:** where tour operators purchase/take over other organisations at the same level within the chain of distribution (i.e. other tour operators).

2 **Vertical integration:** where tour operators purchase/take over other organisations either higher up the chain of distribution (i.e. principals, such as airlines or hotels) or further down the chain (i.e. travel agencies). These are sometimes referred to respectively as backward and forward integration.

There are a number of practical reasons for such integration. Horizontal integration provides a tour operator with:

- economies of scale
- increased market share
- the opportunity to strengthen through expansion
- the opportunity to strengthen through diversification.

Vertical integration provides a tour operator with:

- economies of scale
- continuation of supply
- the ability to control quality
- control over distribution and merchandising.

Evidently, integration is a form of competitive strategy that has been adopted to great effect by the tour operating sector. Therefore, in looking at the structure of the sector (and undertaking assignments or exam questions relating to it) it is worthwhile referring to an appropriate theory as a means of explaining or understanding how and why integration has occurred. Although it is now somewhat dated, Porter's Five Forces model provides a useful basis for the analysis of integration within the tour operating sector (see also Section 13).

While it is important to be able to demonstrate your knowledge of the structure and patterns of ownership of the tour operating sector in assignments or exams, adopting a multidisciplinary approach, by drawing on the theory of competitive strategy in order to explain why extensive concentration and integration has occurred, will undoubtedly impress your examiner.

Tour operations in practice

Not only is there an enormous variety of tour operations, but also tour operators will often adopt different strategies to meet the overall objectives of staying in business and making a profit. Usually, such strategies involve balancing the need to make a profit with market share – typically, smaller operators focus upon developing niche products from which they can achieve higher margins on each holiday sold, whereas larger operators have tended to focus on increasing their market share (i.e. achieving greater capacity), though with lower margins on each holiday sold. Therefore, the type of package holidays an operator develops will be determined by its overall strategic objectives.

Nevertheless, most operators follow a largely similar process in the planning and construction of a package holiday which, depending on the nature of the holiday, may take anything from nine months to three years to complete. There are three stages in the construction of a package holiday:

1 *Stage one.* Research must be undertaken into market trends, existing products and competitive supply, and destination research to establish the feasibility of developing a new product in a new destination.

2 *Stage two.* This involves the actual creation of the package, broadly embracing four areas of activity:

- capacity planning, including both setting target capacity figures and contracting accommodation and aircraft seats
- financial planning, including the critical process of pricing holidays
- sales and marketing, particularly brochure production
- administration, including establishing reservation systems, recruiting resort-based staff and processing initial bookings.

3 *Stage three.* During the first full season, a variety of activities occur, including:

- holiday management
- customer care
- account payment to suppliers.

Challenges facing tour operators

Although tour operators have long enjoyed a dominant position within the travel and tourism industry, they currently face a number of challenges that you need to be aware of. In fact, assignment or exam questions are, perhaps, more likely to focus on these issues as opposed to the practical aspects of tour operations outlined in the previous section. These challenges include:

- the threat of disintermediation linked with advances in information technology.
- competition from no-frills airlines and the subsequent growth in independent travel.
- the need to inject greater quality in the package holiday.
- the need to meet changing customer needs.
- the growing pressure for greater environmental responsibility in tour operations.

Taking it **FURTHER**

There can be no doubting the influential role played by the tour operating sector in the development of international mass tourism. Moreover, as a dynamic and innovative industry, it would appear that, at least in the short term, its future remains reasonably secure despite the challenges posed by, in particular, the Internet and no-frills airlines and the subsequent rise in independent travel. However, in the long term, will tour operating suffer from disintermediation? In other words, will the concept of the package holiday eventually run its course and will the inclusive tour become a minority activity in travel and tourism? It is, therefore, worth considering the potential ways in which tour operators may have to respond to these challenges to maintain their position within the travel and tourism chain of distribution.

Unless your course focuses specifically upon the practice of tour operating, in which case your in-course assessment and/or exam questions may focus on specific aspects of tour operations, you are more likely to be set questions that relate to the structure and influence of, or challenges faced by, the tour operating sector. *In answering any question, however, you are strongly recommended to refer to examples of current tour operators or operations.*

Given the contemporary growth in travel/holiday booking over the Internet, you may well be asked to consider the future of tour operators as intermediaries with the travel and tourism chain of distribution. A typical question would ask:

"Is there a future for tour operators?"

The success of tour operators continues to be based upon the advantages or benefits they offer to both principals and customers. At the same time, however, the Internet has, in principle, reduced the dependency of both principals and tourists on tour operators, while new forms of travel, particularly the no-frills airlines, have removed some of the price advantages enjoyed by tour operators. Nevertheless, the package holiday remains popular, pointing to a number of reasons why tourists will continue to use tour operators rather than travelling independently. Your answer should assess the arguments for and against the likelihood of the decline of tour operations while also referring to the ways in which operators have adapted to the challenge of the Internet.

From an industry structure perspective, questions are likely to focus on the issue of consolidation/integration within the tour operations sector. For example, you may be asked:

"What would be the advantages and disadvantages of further integration within the travel and tourism channel of distribution?"

A particular feature of the tour operating sector in recent years has been the extensive horizontal and vertical integration within the chain of distribution. While such integration has undoubtedly provided the larger tour operators with strategic advantage, it has not always been in the best interests of either destinations or tourists. Therefore, your answer to this question would demonstrate your understanding of the benefits (and also potential costs) of integration to tour operators but would also explore the implications of such integration in the wider context of the tourism system.

Textbook guide

COOPER ET AL. (2005): *Chapter 12*
HOLLOWAY (2002): *Chapter 12*
LAWS (1997)
PENDER (2001): *Chapters 1–4*
SHARPLEY (2002): *Chapter 5*

11
travel and tourism retailing

Strictly speaking, travel and tourism retailing should not be considered a separate or identifiable area of the core curriculum. Travel agents or retailers are, along with tour operators, intermediaries in the tourism system – in fact, in the UK at least, a significant proportion of travel retail outlets are owned by tour operators. Therefore, travel and tourism retailing is usually studied either in tandem with tour operations although, in some cases, it is considered within the broader context of travel distribution. Nevertheless, travel retailers have, for many years, played a vital role in the supply of travel and tourism products and, despite the significant challenges posed by the Internet and the consequential threat of disintermediation, continue to do so. It is, therefore, important to understand the role of the travel retailer in the travel and tourism chain of distribution and, in particular, to be able to assess the future of travel retailing within the tourism system. Indeed, the most common question in this context, and the key theme introduced in this section, is whether there is a future for the travel retailer.

The role of travel retailers

Principals in the travel industry, such as hotels and airlines have various choices for distributing their products. They may, for example, deal directly with the customer through the Internet, sell through a tour operator or use other methods. Hotels, for example, may distribute their products through a group reservation system. Traditionally, however, principals and tour operators have sold their products through travel retailers or, more precisely, travel agents.

The main thing to remember about travel agents is that they are not retailers in the traditional sense. They do not hold any stock and act as agents for their customers only by purchasing products on their behalf from principals or tour operators. Therefore, the contract of sale is not between the customer and travel agent but between the customer and principal.

Therefore, the role of travel retailers within the travel and tourism chain of distribution is to sell a variety of travel products to the general public or, in the case of business travel agencies, to corporate clients. Typically, travel retailers have sold airline tickets, rail/bus tickets, package holidays and hotel rooms, as well as a variety of ancillary products, such as car hire, travel insurance and foreign exchange. For all products sold, retailers receive a commission payment from the principal although, more recently, there has been a move towards reducing levels of commission, particularly for airline tickets.

Travel retailers play a role beyond simply selling travel products. For principals, they provide an effective high-street presence while, for customers, the benefits provided include:

- a 'one-stop' shop on the high street for travel products
- face-to-face service
- access to and comparing a variety of competing products
- access to and, potentially, knowledge of ever-increasing range of products
- in theory, impartial and expert advice or travel counselling, but the counselling role is more common in the USA than in Europe.

A key issue in the debate regarding the future of the travel retail sector is the personal service that they provide and the security of personal contact that cannot be provided by the Internet.

It is important to recognise that some of these benefits are being eroded by the changing nature of travel retailing. In Europe, for example, tour operators offer incentives (higher commission) to meet targets while integration has resulted in **directional selling**. As a result, customers may not receive objective advice and will be provided/left with a limited choice of products.

Types of travel retailers

The traditional all-round travel agency selling a broad variety of products is now a rarity, while the sector is characterised by a different types of outlet. Broadly speaking, there are two main types of travel retailer:

1 *Business travel retailers.* Specialist agencies that meet the particular needs of business clients locally, nationally and internationally. Key organisations to be aware of are American Express and Carlson Wagonlit.

2 *Leisure travel retailers.* This category can be subdivided into:

- holidays hops, typically owned by a tour operator, which concentrate on selling package holidays
- specialist retailers, focusing on particular types of products or markets.

A further characteristic of the sector is the distinction between independent travel retailers and the so-called **multiples**. The sector, particularly in Europe, has become dominated by large chains of travel retailers, often owned by tour operators. These tend to focus on the package holiday market with discounting being the most common means of achieving sales. As a consequence, independent travel retailers frequently combine into alliances, such as consortia or franchise groups, in order to compete with the multiples.

> As with other sectors of the travel and tourism industry, it is easy (and useful) to familiarise yourself with the structure and patterns of ownership within the travel retail sector. Online travel news services or the trade press provide up-to-date information, while accessing major travel organisations' websites is an easy way of learning about their structure and activities.

New competition in the travel retail sector (as, indeed, in high-street retail operations in general) is provided by online travel companies. A number of well-known organisations (Expedia.com, Travelocity.com, Lastminute.com, eBookers.com, etc.) act as virtual travel agencies, as do a large number of more specialist online retailers which focus on particular products or markets.

The economics of travel retailing

The structure and operations of the travel retail sector are largely determined by the economics of travel retailing. An agency's income is derived almost entirely from commission, unless they also sell products such as travel guides or basic travel accessories. As principals have faced greater competition, they have sought ways of reducing distribution costs, including reducing levels of commission and introducing alternative means of paying travel retailers. As a result, all travel retailers have become:

- more commercially oriented
- more cost conscious, cutting training and investment
- focused on higher-commission products
- less able or willing to provide a broad service.

As such, they have moved more to a position of working on behalf of principals rather than, as originally, on behalf of their customers.

The future of travel retailing

As noted above, the key theme in the context of travel retailing is the question of the future of the travel agent. Competition, and the threat of disintermediation, has evolved from:

- principals/tour operators selling direct to the customer
- principals selling/linking to other travel products on their websites
- online booking and ticket-less travel
- the growth of online travel retailers
- an increasingly knowledgeable and experienced travelling public who are happy to book independent travel online.

The end of travel retailing has been forecast for at least a decade, yet the sector has survived, if not flourished. Therefore, the answer to the question about the future of travel retailing may be found by exploring the ways in which the sector has, in reality, responded to the threat of disintermediation.

Taking it **FURTHER**

Travel agents have been an integral part of the travel industry for over a century but their demise has long been forecast. Undoubtedly, information technology has been the greatest threat and the volume of holidays/travel products bought online continues to grow rapidly. Nevertheless, despite the flexibility (and potential price advantages) of online purchasing, most travel retailers are surviving. So, is there likely to be a distinction between what tourists will buy online or over the counter? For holiday purchases, as opposed to flights or other products, do customers still prefer the security of face-to-face transactions?

Inevitably, you will be asked questions that focus on the challenges facing travel agencies/retailers. As a prerequisite, therefore, you should have some knowledge of the structure of the sector, the key players and their activities, as well as being able to demonstrate your understanding of concepts such as disintermediation and dynamic packaging. The broad question – *do travel agencies have a future?* – has become something of an 'old chestnut' and so you are likely to be set more focused questions, such as:

" Critically appraise the extent to which the structure of travel retailing will be determined by the different products sold by different types of retailer. "

Following an introduction to the structural characteristics of travel retailing, the traditional benefits of using travel agents and, in particular, the challenge of online retailing, your answer should explore the extent to which particular products or forms of tourism are more likely to be purchased online, through a holiday shop or at a specialist travel agent. It would then conclude by considering the potential future of the travel retail sector.

An alternative question might be:

" How can independent travel agencies compete with online travel retailers? "

Charting the emergence of online retailers and their increasing market share, your answer should identify the challenges they face and then explore the ways of addressing these challenges. A particular focus would be on the benefits of face-to-face purchasing, though the types of products most likely to be bought (and the associated levels of service required) should be considered, as well as the opportunities for independent retailers themselves to take advantage of information technology in order to sell their products.

Textbook guide

COOPER ET AL. (2005): *Chapter 12*
HOLLOWAY (2002): *Chapter 13*
SHARPLEY (2002): *Chapter 6*

12	
marketing in travel and tourism	

Marketing is a key function in all travel and tourism businesses and organisations. Traditionally it has been seen as the process of identifying and satisfying customers' needs profitably, implying a commercial orientation. However, more recently the value of marketing management to organisations in the public and not-for-profit sectors has been recognised. Consequently, marketing is now considered more generally to be about achieving organisational goals, but specifically with an outward focus on the customer. In short, it is a way of doing business.

Increasingly there appears to be a crossover between the marketing and strategic management functions within organisations. They share many tools and concepts, while the objectives of both seem to be similar. However, a useful distinction is that marketing is usually concerned with short-term, more focused planning, while strategic management takes a more general, long-term perspective. Moreover, strategic management is more concerned with organisational capabilities and external influences, while marketing has the customer as its primary focus.

Of course, marketing is an academic subject in its own right and one which embraces a multitude of sub-themes, such as consumer behaviour, advertising, public relations or branding, as well as numerous types of marketing (for example, database marketing or relationship marketing). There are also many books on marketing, although Philip Kotler is widely seen as the leading author on the subject. Marketing is also ubiquitous on travel and tourism courses and is usually taught as a separate module or unit. However, it is important to realise that marketing permeates, or is related to, almost every aspect of the tourism system; that is, it represents a framework for the study of travel and tourism and most areas of the curriculum, from tourism demand through to visitor management (as well as, of course, the travel industry) can be related to marketing.

Many, if not all, of the running themes in travel and tourism are also relevant to the subject. For example:

1 *Authenticity.* Tourists seek authentic experiences; it is the role of marketing to meet this need.

2 *Sustainable development.* **Societal marketing** is an approach to marketing that embraces social and environmental responsibilities.

3 *Globalisation.* Tourism organisations compete in an increasingly globalised marketplace.

4 *Sociology of tourism.* Understanding the tourist/consumer lies at the heart of tourism marketing.

It is, therefore, vital to have an understanding of marketing and its contribution to the study of travel and tourism. Although most general texts include sections on marketing, you will find it beneficial to read a dedicated travel and tourism marketing book. Kotler et al. apply general marketing principles to tourism and hospitality, but Victor Middleton has long been a key thinker in this area.

Despite the perhaps rather daunting breadth of the subject, the key issues you need to be aware of are as follows.

The nature of the travel and tourism product

Many of the objectives and practices of marketing in travel and tourism are influenced by the nature of the tourism product and, almost always, marketing modules start by exploring the characteristics of tourism. As with most service products, tourism is characterised by:

1 *Perishability*. A service cannot be stored for sale later. An empty hotel bed is lost business.

2 *Heterogeneity/variability*. Each service product, depending on interaction between the provider and consumer, is unique (hence, it is difficult to achieve consistency).

3 *Inseparability*. Services are produced and consumed simultaneously; the product does not exist until it is consumed.

4 *Intangibility*. Services cannot be tested or tried out before purchase, so a sense of trust must be conveyed through the marketing process.

In addition to these generic service characteristics, travel and tourism products in particular are also characterised by:

1 *High fixed costs/low variable costs*. Aeroplanes, hotels and other travel and tourism facilities have high fixed costs – high load factors/occupancy levels must be attained to break even.

2 *Fixed supply capacity*. In the short term, it is difficult to increase or decrease supply.

3 *Complementarity*. Many businesses produce a variety of complementary services that collectively represent the total tourism experience.

These characteristics determine a travel and tourism organisation's approach to marketing. There are two types of marketing:

1   *Tactical marketing*: focusing on short-term problems and solutions, such as reducing the price of a holiday to maintain sales.

2   *Strategic marketing*, focusing on long-term product development, such as introducing new destinations in winter-sun programme.

Successful marketing in travel and tourism depends upon balancing tactical and strategic marketing. For airlines, hotels and tour operators, tactical marketing (utilising tools such as yield management) is a vital activity to ensure remaining capacity is sold. At the same time, however, long-term strategic marketing is also necessary to develop new products or brands so that the organisation remains competitive.

The tourist and market segmentation

Given marketing's primary focus on the consumer, understanding tourist/consumer behaviour is fundamental to marketing in travel and tourism. It is, therefore, important to understand the tourism demand process, **tourist typologies**, and **tourist motivation**, themes that are covered in Sections 3 and 4. The purpose of developing an understanding of tourist/consumer behaviour is to help identify **market segments**.

Travel and tourism markets can be segmented in different ways or according to different variables. For example:

- Demographic variables: for example age, social class, family stage.
- Psychographic variables: for example, allocentrics or psychocentrics, or values/lifestyle measures.
- Product benefits: adventure tourism, for example, attracts tourists seeking particular experiences.

An interesting way of looking at segmentation in practice is to select a large tour operator and compare the different holiday brochures it offers. The picture on the front will immediately reveal the market segment at which the brochure is targeted, and this will be confirmed by the type, location and cost of holidays included in the brochure.

The marketing mix

The concept of the **marketing mix** is fundamental to marketing. As the basis of marketing planning, it represents the variables or tools employed and manipulated by an organisation to achieve its marketing objectives. Traditionally, the marketing mix is considered in terms of the so-called four 'Ps':

1 *Product:* what is actually experienced by the tourist, a bundle of benefits that includes tangible and intangible elements. The concept of **core** and **augmented product** is also of relevance. Increasingly, service quality management has become an important challenge for marketing management in travel and tourism.

2 *Price:* the amount of money tourists pay for the product. In travel and tourism, price is a powerful tactical weapon to stimulate demand, particularly where there are many competitive or substitute products.

3 *Place:* traditionally, the point of sale where a product is inspected and purchased. In travel and tourism, place generally refers to the distribution system rather than the destination, the latter being the product. Tourism businesses need to create methods by which tourists can easily purchase travel and tourism products prior to consumption (i.e. in the generating region). Information technology has had a significant influence on place.

4 *Promotion:* the methods by which products and their prices are communicated to potential customers, such as advertising, public relations, sales promotions, direct mail, etc. Increasingly, communication methods seek to gain feedback from customers.

In addition, it is suggested that another three 'Ps' should be considered in the marketing mix for service products:

1 *People/performers:* services are provided (and received) by people, so employees, customers and others who might influence the enjoyment of the tourism experience (local people, other tourists) should be included in the mix.

2 *Process:* the process through which services are delivered, including service recovery where problems occur.

3 *Physical evidence:* elements that introduce a tangible element to the service, such as uniforms, music, etc.

It is useful to think of the four (or seven!) 'Ps' as a set of tools that collectively determine the marketing process. Middleton uses the analogy of a car – coordinating steering, braking, accelerating and changing gears helps the driver to get where he or she wants to go.

The marketing process

The marketing process, sometimes referred to as marketing planning, is the ongoing process of planning, implementing, controlling and monitoring marketing. The marketing plan is a specific, written statement which is the outcome of the marketing process at a particular point in time.

The marketing process follows a number of stages not dissimilar to the stages inherent in strategic management (see Section 13). These stages can be thought of as four questions:

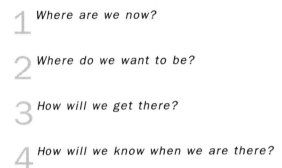

1 *Where are we now?*

2 *Where do we want to be?*

3 *How will we get there?*

4 *How will we know when we are there?*

These questions can be translated into a number of consecutive tasks or activities:

- setting objectives/mission statement
- marketing audit: market research, internal/external audits
- development of marketing strategies
- identification and evaluation of alternative plans/mixes
- marketing programme (implementation)
- monitoring and review.

As noted earlier, marketing is an essential function for all travel and tourism business and organisations. Different types of organisations will have different objectives and will, therefore, follow different marketing processes and develop different marketing plans. Nevertheless, a customer focus and manipulation of the marketing mix remain key concepts for all marketing contexts. At the same time, there are three key issues to consider for the future of travel and tourism marketing:

1 *Branding.* Within the travel industry, and also for destinations, branding has emerged as a powerful marketing tool.

2 *The environment.* The development of responsible, sustainable or environmentally sound tourism products has long been a tourism planning objective. Therefore, societal marketing will become of increasing importance.

3 *Service quality.* An increase in value/quality-conscious tourists and consumer protection legislation as well as an increasingly competitive marketplace will require a greater focus on quality in travel and tourism marketing.

Taking it **FURTHER**

Marketing has traditionally been concerned with meeting customers' needs profitably. In other words, for commercial organisations it has been a means of achieving organisational profit objectives through providing customers with what they want, when they want it and at the right price. More recently, marketing has evolved into a broader process for the achievement of objectives in all kinds of organisations, though still focusing principally on the needs of the customer. However, within the tourism industry, the principal purpose of marketing is, arguably, to make a profit, with organisations seeking to develop new products, experiences and brands to remain competitive. Is it likely, therefore, that marketing in travel and tourism will take account of broader issues, such as ethics, social responsibility or environmental concerns?

Given the breadth of marketing as a subject, it is difficult to predict the sort of questions that you are likely to be asked in exams. In fact, as with all areas of travel and tourism, the way in which the topic has been presented to you in lectures should indicate the particular themes that will come up. Nevertheless, it is likely that you will be asked questions that relate directly or indirectly to the key issues that have been identified in this section. For example, with regard to the marketing process, you may be asked to:

"Compare how the marketing process varies in public, private and voluntary sector organisations in travel and tourism."

The marketing process starts with the identification of organisational objectives, which vary considerably across travel and tourism organisations. Identifying different types of organisations within the tourism system and drawing on examples in practice, from commercial operators (hotels, airlines, etc.), destinations, marketing bodies or museums through to conservation organisations or pressure groups, your answer should highlight their different objectives, the challenges they face and the resultant marketing philosophy/process adopted.

A more specific question might be:

66 Critically appraise the importance of branding in the marketing of travel and tourism products. 99

Branding has become an important tool in the marketing of all products, including travel and tourism. After defining branding and exploring its contribution to effective marketing in general, answers should relate this to specific sectors of travel and tourism, and how it helps to meet some of the challenges posed by the typical characteristics of service products.

A key theme in travel and tourism has long been the concept of sustainable tourism development. Therefore, questions frequently focus on this topic. For example:

66 Consider the role of marketing in achieving sustainable tourism development. 99

Achieving sustainable development is the responsibility of all organisations within the tourism system. In principle, the adoption of a societal/environmental approach to marketing, utilising the marketing mix to develop and promote sustainable forms of tourism, may contribute to the achievement of sustainable development, although the size, diversity and fragmentation of the industry remains a significant challenge. Moreover, although marketing undoubtedly influences *what* products tourists may buy, it is uncertain to what extent it can influence *how* they consume it.

Textbook guide

COOPER ET AL. **(2005):** *Chapters 15 to 18*
HOLLOWAY **(2004)**
HORNER AND SWARBROOKE **(1996)**
KOTLER ET AL. **(2002)**
PENDER AND SHARPLEY **(2005):** *Chapter 7*
SEATON AND BENNETT **(1996)**

13

strategy in travel and tourism

Any business or organisation, whether in the private, public or 'voluntary' (i.e. not-for-profit) sector, should undertake strategic planning and management. Without strategy, organisations are liable to suffer from **strategic drift** resulting from a failure to recognise and respond to the changing external environment. As a consequence, they may encounter difficulty in meeting their objectives, become less competitive or, as occurs occasionally (and sometimes spectacularly!) in travel and tourism, ultimately fail or go out of business.

Thus, strategic management is, perhaps, the most important activity undertaken by any organisation. It is also an area of academic study in its own right and is commonly taught on travel and tourism courses. Surprisingly, however, there are very few texts that apply the concepts of strategic management to the specific context of travel and tourism – two key textbooks are Tribe (1997) and Evans et al. (2003) – although there are many general texts on strategy. Perhaps the most widely used of these is Johnson and Scholes' *Exploring Corporate Strategy.*

Irrespective of the context or focus of a strategic management unit or course, the same basic principles and concepts apply. You may, therefore, find it useful to refer to one of the standard texts on strategy in order to develop your understanding of the subject.

When studying strategy for travel and tourism, there are two points you should be immediately aware of:

1 The principles of strategic management apply to all types of organisations, not just commercial businesses. Therefore, although strategy is most frequently studied in the context of sectors of the travel and tourism industry, such as airlines, tour operators or accommodation, it is of equal importance to other types of organisation, such as **national tourist boards** or destination management organisations.

2 The concepts and principles of strategic management are not prescriptive solutions to problems; rather, they are in effect a set of tools that can help organisations to recognise and understand the challenges they face, and to devise appropriate responses.

At the conceptual level, strategy is a rather 'dry' subject. You should, therefore, always try to use examples from the travel and tourism industry to bring your assignments or exam answers to life. The airline industry in general, and the no-frills sector in particular, is a very fruitful source for examples of effective (and ineffective) strategy in practice, while many destination tourism development policies often follow the principles of strategic planning and management.

What, then, is strategy for travel and tourism all about? Essentially, though simplistically, it is a process through which travel and tourism organisations decide upon where they want to be in the future and the most appropriate or effective means of getting there. There are four common elements of successful strategy:

1 Simple, consistent and long-term goals.

2 A clear understanding of the external or competitive environment.

3 An objective appraisal of internal resources.

4 The effective implementation of the chosen strategy.

These reflect the four key stages or elements of strategic management:

1 Establishing long-term goals (the mission).

2 Strategic analysis.

3 Strategic choice.

4 Strategic implementation.

Key to understanding the subject is your ability to identify these stages and to apply the relevant models or concepts at each stage.

> It is important to remember that strategy is a process. That is, it is not a one-off activity but something that should be ongoing, particularly in a highly dynamic and competitive industry such as travel and tourism that operates in an equally dynamic and uncertain environment.

Establishing goals/mission

Organisations cannot begin to develop strategy without a clear goal or aim. This is normally articulated in the organisation's mission statement, the purpose of which is to communicate the objectives, purpose and values of the organisation to all stakeholders. The mission statement will reflect the nature of the organisation (private/commercial, public sector, voluntary) and will be influenced by who the organisation exists for. Stakeholder analysis is a useful means of assessing why particular organisational goals are established. A mission statement may also be supported by a set of objectives representing measurable long-term targets upon which achievement of the mission depends.

Strategic analysis

Strategic analysis is concerned with the identification and assessment of the principal factors that will influence the ability of the organisation to achieve its long-term goals. It may be alternatively described as a SWOT analysis:

S – organisational **s**trengths
W – organisational **w**eaknesses
O – external **o**pportunities
T – external **t**hreats.

SWOT analysis is a useful, compact and clear means of identifying the internal strengths and weaknesses and external opportunities and threats. However, it is important to remember that it is no more than a summary of key factors that emerge from more detailed strategic analysis – it should result from, not replace, other more specific analyses.

Thus, strategic analysis embraces two areas of concern: an internal analysis of the organisation and an external analysis of the environment within which it operates.

Internal strategic analysis focuses on three key areas:

1 *Resources*, which can be categorised under three headings.

- tangible resources (i.e. physical resources and financial resources)
- intangible resources (i.e. knowledge, skills, reputation, brands, etc.)
- human resources.

2 *Competencies* (or capabilities), which are a collection of attributes that develop from the organisation's resources and which enable it to operate within its industry or sector; and core competencies, which are attributes specific to an organisation that enable it to out-perform other, similar organisations. Core competencies arise from more effective use of competencies and resources, and provide the organisation with competitive advantage.

3 *Performance measures*, which evaluate financial performance, human resources performance and product performance. The latter includes a number of evaluation tools, including:

- value chain analysis assesses which activities provide greatest value to the product
- product life cycle analysis predicts the development of a product
- portfolio analysis assesses products in terms of market share and market growth. A widely used model is the Boston Consulting Group matrix (BCG).

External strategic analysis focuses on two areas:

1 The macro-environment, which is the broad environment within which the organisation's industry and markets exist. With reference to the running theme of the tourism system, the

macro-environment is, therefore, the external global environment within which travel and tourism occurs. A variety of acronyms are used to list the different external influences that should be assessed, including PEST, STEP, and PESTLE analysis. The most extended framework suggested in travel and tourism is SCEPTICAL, standing for:

Social
Cultural
Economic
Physical
Technical
International
Communications and infrastructure
Administrative and institutional
Legal and political.

> *Macro-environment analysis is a useful tool that can be applied to many areas of travel and tourism and, even in a simpler form, such as STEP, provides a valuable framework for answering assignment or exam questions on, for example, destination planning, global tourism flows, risk and crisis management, and so on.*

2 The micro-environment, which is the immediate industry environment, embracing competitors, suppliers and customers. It is often referred to as competitive analysis and the most commonly used model is Porter's Five Forces model, which suggests there are Five Forces or influences which determine the level of competition within an industry. These forces are:

- the threat of new entrants to the industry
- the threat of substitute products
- the power of buyers or customers
- the power of suppliers
- the degree of rivalry between competitors.

Strategic choice

Strategic choice focuses on developing different strategic options, evaluating these options, and the selection of the most appropriate option. Within this process there are three key concepts:

1 *Competitive strategy.* Porter developed a widely-cited generic strategy framework based on cost-leadership or differentiation strategy. This has been criticised in the travel and tourism context, particularly as organisations may adopt a hybrid strategy (low cost and differentiated), while an alternative framework is based upon quality and price as strategic options.

2 *Strategic direction.* Organisations should decide upon the direction of development. Four choices of growth strategies are suggested by Ansoff's product-market framework:

- market penetration
- market development
- product development
- diversification.

Alternative strategic directions include stability strategies (consolidation) and retrenchment strategies.

3 *Strategic methods.* The method of strategic development is critical to the success of strategy. The different methods of developing strategy are:

- organic/internal growth
- mergers/take-overs
- collaborative arrangements: strategic alliances, joint ventures, franchising, etc.

Strategic methods are of particular relevance to the travel and tourism industry, with different sectors favouring different methods. It is well worth considering why, for example, strategic alliances are popular within the airline sector, franchising is common within the accommodation sector, and take-overs have been dominant within the tour operating sector.

Prior to strategic choices being made, each strategic option must be evaluated. Typical criteria for evaluation are:

1 **Suitability.** Does the strategy exploit opportunities, avoid threats and capitalise on the organisation's strengths?

2 **Feasibility.** Is the strategy realistic in terms of available resources and competitor reactions?

3 **Acceptability.** Does the strategy meet the needs of the stakeholders?

Strategic implementation

The final stage in strategic management is putting the chosen strategy into action. Three key questions must be addressed:

1 How will the strategy be resourced? Attention needs to be paid to financial, human, physical and technological resource requirements.

2 What impact will the strategy have on organisational structure and culture?

3 How will the resultant organisational change be managed?

The study of strategic management is both broad and complex. While it is important to be aware of the different stages in the strategic management process and to understand the contribution of different models and concepts to that process, it is more useful to be able to apply your understanding of the process to specific contexts, sectors or challenges within travel and tourism.

Taking it **FURTHER**

The basis of 'traditional' strategic management is the concept of gaining competitive advantage; that is, strategy is concerned with competing with, and doing better than, other organisations in the sector. It is, therefore, about competition and 'winning' – gaining greater market share, out-performing the competition financially, and so on. More recently, however, academics have been concerned with the extent to which collaboration, as opposed to competition, is a more appropriate basis for achieving strategic success. Within the airline sector, for example, strategic alliances have proved to be a successful strategy. It may be time, therefore, to begin to rethink our approach to strategic management.

There are two ways in which exam questions may be focused. First, they may be presented in such a way as to give you the opportunity to demonstrate your overall knowledge/understanding of strategic management, whereby you would use examples/issues from travel and tourism to illustrate or exemplify your answers. For example, a general question would be:

"Why should all travel and tourism organisations undertake strategic management, and what are the key features of successful strategy?"

Strategic management enables organisations to meet their long-term goals by matching, or achieving strategic fit, between its resources/competencies and its external environment. Your answer would define the meaning and purpose of strategy and explain the different stages/elements of the strategic management process, using examples from different travel and tourism organisations to highlight the importance of each element.

Second, you may be asked to assess the challenges facing particular sectors of the industry, utilising the concepts or theories of strategy to underpin your answers. This might be in the form of the analysis of a case study of which you are already aware (airlines, major tour operators or international hotel chains are often the subject of such case studies) – in fact, strategy for travel and tourism units are frequently assessed by way of coursework that requires a strategic analysis of a particular travel and tourism business or organisation. Whether as an exam question or as an assignment, a logical analysis of the organisation's activities following the stages/models of strategic management would enable you to produce a well-structured answer and the opportunity to propose your own ideas for the organisation's future strategy. Alternatively, you might be asked to compare different organisations from a strategic perspective. For example:

"How do the strategic challenges facing an international airline, a tour operator and a national tourist board differ?"

Strategic management is of equal importance for each type of organisation, yet their challenges and strategic responses will differ according to their goals/mission and, in particular, their external opportunities and threats.

Textbook guide

EVANS, CAMPBELL AND STONEHOUSE **(2003)**
JOHNSON AND SCHOLES **(2002)**
PENDER AND SHARPLEY **(2005):** *Chapter 8*
TRIBE **(1997)**

14	
economics of travel and tourism	

There are two ways of looking at the economics of travel and tourism. Most commonly, and linked to the potential contribution of travel and tourism to national or regional development (see Section 15), the focus is upon what textbooks often refer to as the economic impacts of tourism, or the economic benefits and costs of tourism development, and the means of measuring them. In economics, this perspective is referred to as **macro-economics**. Conversely, tourism economics can also be considered at the level of individual businesses or tourists, an approach known as **micro-economics**.

When studying travel and tourism, both perspectives are of value. While the macro-economic approach is essential in assessing the economic benefits and costs of tourism development (with evident links to the running theme of sustainable development), micro-economic analysis provides, for example, an extra dimension to the understanding of the demand for travel and tourism as well as a basis for exploring the economics of, say, the accommodation sector. Most general tourism textbooks tend to adopt the macro focus, though the specialist texts by Bull (1995) and Tribe (2004) also embrace micro-economics. If you have a particular interest in this area, then the academic journal *Tourism Economics* is also well worth looking at.

Do not be put off by the term 'economics'! You do not have to be an economist to understand the economics of travel and tourism, and the economic concepts that are applied to travel and tourism are relatively simple to grasp.

Essentially, economics is concerned with how a balance can be achieved between, on the one hand, scarce resources and, on the other hand, the demand for those resources. In other words, resources (other than those that are 'free', such as air) are finite and tend to be limited in supply relative to demand. Thus, economics is basically concerned with the problems of choice resulting from this scarcity of resources.

Micro-economics

At the micro-economic level, this issue is manifested in the relationship between demand and supply. All individuals demand goods and services (including tourism); the total demand for a particular product is what the industry must supply if all customers are to be satisfied. In reality, demand and supply are rarely matched and the resulting interaction between the two is determined by price. The basic economic rules of demand and supply for any product, including tourism, are:

- As the price falls, demand will rise; as the price rises, demand will fall.
- As the price rises, the quantity supplied will rise; as the price falls, supply will also fall.

In practice, of course, there are a variety of factors other than price that affect demand. In other words, conditions of demand may alter the position of the **demand curve**. The aggregate, or total, demand for travel and tourism may be determined by a variety of economic factors, including:

- levels of personal disposable income
- holiday entitlements
- promotion of the destination
- exchange rates
- comparison between home and destination prices.

Moreover, demand is also influenced by the relationship between competing products and their prices. In tourism, there may be substitute products, where an increase in the demand for one product may lead to a fall in demand for another product, and complements, where increasing demand for one will stimulate a similar increase in demand for the other. Substitutes may be normal or inferior products – as income falls, consumers may switch to inferior substitutes, such as cheaper holidays or economy class as opposed to business class airline seats.

An interesting exercise is to consider all the economic (and non-economic) factors that influence aggregate demand to a particular destination and the resultant importance of price.

The supply of a product, or the position of the **supply curve**, can also be influenced by a variety of factors, including:

- the price of competing products
- the cost of providing the product
- barriers to entry and exit
- government regulations.

Supply and demand can be brought together through the price mechanism, a process whereby economic decisions in the economy are determined by the workings of the market. In theory, the market works to create a condition of equilibrium, where the volume demanded and the volume supplied are the same. For example, where the price of a package holiday is too high, so that supply outstrips demand, either supply must be reduced or the price must be reduced to stimulate demand.

A common strategy among tour operators is to either offer discounts for early bookings and/or to implement yield management processes to sell off excess capacity as the date of the holiday approaches. This is simply a manifestation of the price mechanism to ensure that supply matches demand (i.e. so that the operator sells all its holidays).

In the context of micro-economics, you should also be aware of the concept of **elasticity of demand** or **supply**. Where demand is very responsive to small changes in price, then demand is elastic; conversely, where demand is unaffected by changes in price, the demand is inelastic. For example, summer-sun package holidays (usually with many substitutes) tend to be price elastic. Conversely, specialist or luxury products, with more limited supply and few substitutes, tend to be price inelastic.

Macro-economics: the impacts of tourism

Given its scale as both a social and economic activity, it is inevitable that travel and tourism has significant impacts on destination environments and societies. An understanding of these impacts is essential to the study of travel and tourism.

> The word 'impact' has negative connotations and, frequently, the so-called 'negative' impacts of tourism are highlighted, particularly in the popular media. However, travel and tourism brings many benefits to destinations (and generating regions) and it is, therefore, better to think in terms of consequences rather than impacts.

The main reason that destinations seek to develop travel and tourism is for the potential economic benefits it can bring. These benefits should, ideally, outweigh any costs or disadvantages of developing tourism so that, like any business, the destination makes a 'profit'. Indeed, many countries have policies to support tourism as a potentially valuable sector of the economy.

Different destinations are more or less able to take economic advantage of travel and tourism. The extent to which economic benefits are realised is determined by a variety of factors:

- the nature of tourist sites and facilities and their attraction to tourists
- the volume of tourist expenditure at the destination
- the level of economic development of the destination
- the extent of local economic diversification
- the extent to which the economy is dependent on the imports of goods, services and capital.

> As a general rule, developed modern countries/economies are better able to benefit from tourism than less developed countries/economies.

The development of travel and tourism brings both economic benefits and costs. The economic benefits are:

1 *Foreign exchange earnings/contribution to the balance of payments.* For many destination countries, international tourism is a vital export sector.

2 *Economic diversification.* Tourism is seen as an effective means of achieving economic regeneration or diversification in both urban and rural areas.

3 *Income generation.* Travel and tourism is an important source of government revenues, while direct tourism expenditure (i.e. tourist receipts) stimulates further expenditure (hence, income for local businesses) through the multiplier effect.

4 *Employment.* Globally, travel and tourism is a major employer (directly and indirectly), though attention must be paid to the nature of local employment in the sector.

It is important to distinguish between tourism receipts, which represent direct tourist expenditure in a destination, and the tourism economy, which represents the total direct and indirect value of tourism to a destination. The latter is difficult to measure, although **Tourism Satellite Accounting** is increasingly used as a means of measuring the overall economic benefits of tourism. The WTTC publishes satellite accounts for most destinations on its website.

The development of travel and tourism may also result in economic costs for a destination. Therefore, the true economic contribution of tourism must be seen in terms of net benefits. Tourism receipts data, such those that published by the WTO, hide the extent of these economic costs, which include:

1 *Leakages.* A proportion of the income from tourism is spent on importing goods to meet tourists' needs.

2 *Higher import costs.* As the wealth of a destination increases, local people demand other goods that must be imported.

3 *Inflation.* Frequently, land/property prices increase in popular tourism areas, while the costs of local goods and services may also increase.

4 *Opportunity costs.* Travel and tourism may not, in the long term, be the most effective development option (although in many cases there may be no other option).

5 *External costs.* These include the costs of refuse collection, extra policing, health services and so on.

Taking it **FURTHER**

> The economic value of travel and tourism to destinations has been tradition-
> ally seen in terms of tourism receipts or, more recently, in terms of the
> tourism economy. Thus, the net economic benefit of tourism to a destination
> can, in theory at least, be calculated in terms of direct and indirect expendi-
> ture on goods and services minus costs, such as imports. However, many of
> the attractions that tourists enjoy are, in a sense, free – the sea, the climate,
> and the local environment, for example, contribute to the tourism experience.
> As a result, the local economy does not benefit from the use of these
> resources. Though the issue is complex, is there a case for valuing these 'free'
> resources and passing on the costs of their use to tourists and the benefits
> of their use to local communities?

Exam questions are likely to focus either on the application of micro-
economic theory to the demand for/supply of travel and tourism, or
the macro-economic study and measurement of tourism's impacts. An
example of the former might be:

" Critically appraise the economic factors that may influence the demand for tourism. "

Basic economic theory suggests that as the price falls, demand will rise.
However, within the context of travel and tourism, a variety of economic factors
other than price will determine the demand for travel and tourism. These factors
may relate to the tourist/the generating region, the destination, or a comparison
between the two. Attention should also be drawn to the concept of price elasticity related to the nature of tourism products.

The principal reason for developing tourism is its potential economic
contribution to destination areas. Therefore, questions frequently focus
on understanding and measuring that contribution. For example:

" Consider the extent to which tourist receipt statistics provide an accurate picture of the economic benefits of travel and tourism to a destination. "

The economic impact of tourism is most frequently cited in terms of tourist receipts. However, these do not reveal the potential costs of developing travel and tourism or the effects of indirect expenditure. Drawing on examples, your answer should explore the full extent of these costs and benefits, referring to processes such as Tourism Satellite Accounting. The conclusion must be that caution should be exercised in promoting (and calculating) the economic benefits of travel and tourism.

A more specific question in this area might be:

❝ How effective is the tourism multiplier concept as a means of calculating the value of travel and tourism? ❞

There are a number of types of tourism multipliers, as well as a variety of ways of calculating them. Although widely used, however, there are a number of difficulties in calculating multiplier values as well as a number of weaknesses, such as problems of data collection. Highlighting these issues, your answer should argue that multipliers can provide a more realistic picture of the economic value of travel and tourism, although actual multiplier values should be treated with caution.

Textbook guide

BULL **(1995)**
COOPER ET AL. **(2005):** *Chapter 5*
SHARPLEY **(2002):** *Chapter 17*
TRIBE **(2004)**

15	
tourism and development	

One of the most important things you should remember when studying travel and tourism is that the development of tourism is not an end in itself but, rather, a means to an end. In other words, tourism is not developed and promoted for its own sake, but because it is widely considered to be an effective means of achieving social and economic development in destination areas. Certainly, most textbooks identify this developmental role for tourism, highlighting its contribution to income, foreign exchange earnings and employment, while tourism figures prominently in the development policies of many countries.

Not surprisingly, perhaps, most attention is paid to the role of tourism in less developed countries. However, the reason for developing tourism in developed, industrialised countries, whether in cities, at the seaside or in the countryside, is exactly the same – its contribution to development and regeneration.

All too often, however, this developmental role of travel and tourism is taken for granted. That is, little attention is paid to *how* tourism contributes to development – how the developmental needs of the destination can be best met by tourism and even what development actually is. If you are able to think about some of these questions, then you will be able to demonstrate a much deeper understanding of the role of tourism in national and international development – although you will probably find that there are few answers to the questions!

Underpinning the study of tourism and development is the discipline of development studies, sometimes seen as a branch of economics. Recently, a number of tourism academics have begun to explore the link between tourism and development studies (see the textbook guide below) but you may also find it interesting to browse through development studies books in your library – being able to refer to these in your assignments or essays will certainly impress your examiner.

Don't forget – most textbooks or academic journal articles have extensive reference lists. If you want to discover the main sources or find out who the key writers on the subject are, it's always a good idea to look at reference lists first.

Exploring tourism and development is not about planning; it is about taking a step back and thinking about some key issues and questions that should be considered before the planning process starts. The first of these is: why is tourism seen as an effective development tool?

Why tourism?

As many academics observe, tourism is for many places an option of last resort. In other words, they simply have no choice other than to develop tourism. Nevertheless, there are a number of reasons why tourism is favoured:

- It is a growth industry.
- It redistributes wealth.
- It provides opportunities for **backward linkages** in the local economy.
- It uses natural, 'free' resources and infrastructure.
- It does not, in principle, face any trade barriers.
- It can promote environmental protection.
- It provides facilities for local people as well as tourists.

But, what is development?

Academics talk about tourism contributing to development (and we all think we have an idea what the term means) but it is, in fact, quite difficult to define. It is also important, of course, to have some idea of what development is, if nothing else so that we can measure how successful tourism is in achieving or contributing to it. From a definitional perspective, development was originally seen (and measured) in economic terms; that is, economic growth was synonymous with development (and, in a tourism context, perhaps still is). However, the meaning of development has expanded considerably, now embracing not only economic opportunities and growth but also social benefits and facilities, political freedom and cultural factors, such as esteem and self-identity. The extent to which these are being achieved is measured by a variety of indices, including life expectancy, education, access to clean water, and so on (a useful example being the United Nation Development Programme's annual Human Development Index). However, it does become difficult to see how tourism can contribute to all of these developmental needs.

In trying to understand what development is, think about the other side of the coin – that is, underdevelopment. Identifying the typical characteristics of a less developed country points to what the objectives of development are. A good source of information is the United Nations Development Programme website: www.undp.org.

Theories of development

Just as the meaning of development had changed over time, so too have the so-called 'paradigms' or theories of development. While you do not need to have an in-depth understanding of these, you will certainly benefit from having a grasp of the basics – it will provide you with a theoretical foundation for explaining how tourism may, or may not, contribute to development, as well as helping to explain what the dominant (and running) theme in travel and tourism, namely, sustainable tourism development, is all about.

Essentially, there are four theories of development that you need to be aware of:

1 *Modernisation theory*. This suggests that all countries/ societies eventually become 'modern' and that the process of becoming modern can be speeded up by the introduction of an economic sector, such as tourism, which stimulates other sectors of the economy. This is a useful means of explaining the development of resorts as a vehicle for wider development of the destination area.

2 *Dependency theory*. Essentially, underdevelopment in some countries is caused or maintained by their dependent relationship with (and exploitation by) other, richer countries. The political economy of the international tourism system is considered by some to be a manifestation of dependency theory.

3 *Economic neoliberalism.* This refers to international lending programmes that require recipient countries to liberalise their economies. This has often resulted in a worsening of local conditions.

4 *Alternative development.* Contrasting with the other three theories which promote economic growth, alternative development represents a 'bottom-up', grassroots approach to development which focuses upon the satisfaction of people's basic needs. Importantly, alternative development provides the basis for the concept of sustainable development, which has environmental sustainability at its core.

Given the importance attached to sustainable tourism development both in the literature and in practice, it is vital that you familiarise yourself with the concept and the debates surrounding it. The *Journal of Sustainable Tourism* is well worth looking at in this context, as are the numerous textbooks that deal with the subject.

> Frequently, sustainable tourism development is looked at in only environmental terms – that is, sustainable tourism development is seen as tourism that is environmentally friendly. However, it is important not to forget the developmental dimension. Ideally, tourism should contribute to a destination's broader sustainable development.

Sustainable development and tourism

The basic objective of sustainable tourism development is to achieve a balance between the tourism environment, the needs of local communities and the needs of tourists. In other words, sustainable tourism development is concerned with achieving, through tourism:

- developmental objectives: focusing on basic needs, 'bottom-up', locally controlled development
- environmental/sustainability objectives: conserving/protecting the environment, particularly conserving non-renewable resources.

However, the very nature of travel and tourism suggests that these objectives are difficult to achieve. The debate is complex and varied, but the issues to think about are:

- the structure, scale and diversity of the tourism industry
- the political economy of global tourism
- the nature of tourism consumption.

In short, there are a number of 'truths' about tourism, usefully summarised by Bob McKercher in an article in the *Journal of Sustainable Tourism,* that must be considered when thinking about the potential of sustainable tourism development.

Tourism's role in development

The last question to be asked is, how can tourism contribute to development? While sustainable tourism development has been the most favoured approach for a number of years (and one adopted in may countries and destinations), more recently it has become accepted that there is no single, 'right' way of developing tourism. In other words, there is no single model of tourism development.

There are three key issues to be considered when looking at how tourism may contribute to development:

1 *The nature of the destination.* Tourist destinations are infinitely variable. From a tourism development perspective, a widely cited model that you need to be aware of is Richard Butler's 'Tourism Area Life Cycle' model which, similar to the marketing concept of a product life cycle, suggests that destinations progress through a number of stages, from exploration to stagnation/decline or rejuvenation. At the same time, however, destinations are defined by:

- physical/environmental characteristics: urban, rural, wilderness, etc.
- socio-cultural characteristics
- economic characteristics.

Each of these may determine the approach to tourism development that is most appropriate.

2 *Government/governance.* The degree or type of government control will influence the nature of tourism development in a destination. A commonly cited example of government-induced resort development (following the principles of modernisation theory) is Cancún in Mexico.

3 *The tourism industry.* A key factor in the nature of tourism development is the approach of the travel and tourism industry itself. Different organisations or businesses in travel and tourism have varying approaches to environmental concern, developing appropriate forms of tourism, working with local communities, and so on, while the profit motive of most businesses may conflict with broader destinational development goals. A number of types of tourism, such as ecotourism or **pro-poor tourism**, are currently in vogue, though it is worth considering the extent to which these contribute effectively to the socio-economic (or sustainable) development of destinations.

> *Although tourism is widely considered to be an effective means of achieving development (and there are many examples of destinations, regions or countries that have benefited significantly from the growth and development of tourism), it is important to remember that tourism alone cannot promote social and economic development. Its major role, perhaps, is to stimulate economic growth.*

Taking it **FURTHER**

Sustainable tourism development has dominated tourism planning and development since the early 1990s. This is, perhaps, not surprising given the wider support for sustainable development as the contemporary approach to international development, as well as ever-increasing concern for the impacts of tourism, particularly mass tourism, on destination environments and societies. However, it is now recognised that sustainable tourism development may not always be the best approach to tourism development – in fact, in some circumstances, the development of 'traditional', mass tourism may be more beneficial to destinations than forms of sustainable tourism development.

Questions on the relationship between tourism and development will almost certainly focus on the ways in which the contribution of travel and tourism to development in destinational areas can be optimised. As a minimum, you should be able to discuss the meaning of development and, where relevant, to refer to appropriate development theories. As always, it is also useful to be familiar with, and to be able to draw upon, the tourism development process that has occurred in different destinations.

One of the major issues is the role of the travel and tourism industry itself. You may be asked, therefore:

❝ How can the travel and tourism industry contribute to sustainable development in destination areas? ❞

Achieving sustainable development through tourism faces a number of challenges, not least the nature and characteristics of the travel and tourism industry. Identifying the prerequisites for sustainable tourism development, your answer should identify the ways in which the structure and operations of the industry may militate against sustainable development, focusing in particular on the political economy of tourism. You should then explore ways in which the industry, both in principle and in practice, might play a more positive role in promoting sustainable development.

More generally, the concept of sustainable development remains the subject of intense debate. A possible question in this context may be:

❝ Critically appraise the potential for sustainable tourism development. ❞

This question can be approached in a number of ways. However, as a starting point the meaning, principles and objectives of sustainable tourism development should be identified, as should its potential for minimising travel and tourism's negative impacts and optimising its contribution to development. The challenges facing it should then be explored and the fact that different destinations face different developmental needs. Your answer should conclude that, under certain circumstances, sustainable tourism development is a viable approach, but that different models of development may be more appropriate in different circumstances.

Textbook guide

OPPERMAN AND CHON **(1997):** *Chapters 1 and 2*
PEARCE **(1989):** *Chapter 1*
PENDER AND SHARPLEY **(2005):** *Chapter 13*
SHARPLEY AND TELFER **(2002):** *Chapters 1 and 2*

16	
planning travel and tourism	

Effective tourism development does not happen by accident. In other words, the fundamental role of tourism is to contribute to the social and economic development of destination areas. If this is to occur, then tourism must be planned so that, beyond providing satisfying experiences for tourists, destinations themselves benefit while the potential costs – the economic, socio-cultural and environmental impacts – are minimised.

It is, then, easy to justify both the need for planning in tourism (and there are plenty of examples in practice of poor or a lack of planning) and also the importance of studying it as part of a travel and tourism course. However, this planning process itself is in reality rather more complex:

- Planning occurs at different levels within the tourism system, from the development of a site or attraction, through destination planning, to regional or national planning. At each level it becomes more complex, while the objectives may also differ.
- A variety of organisations, each with their own objectives, may be involved in the planning process.
- Tourism planning will vary according to the specific needs or characteristics of different destinations and types of tourism.

Consequently, the study of the subject is usually concerned with broader issues relating to the tourism planning process in general rather than focusing on specific contexts or destinations.

There is no single planning process in travel and tourism. Planning must respond to the specific characteristics and needs of individual destinations and, therefore, as a student of travel and tourism, you need to be aware of the role, objectives and process of planning and be able to apply these to different contexts.

What is planning?

Although it may seem an easy question to answer, it is important that you are clear in your own mind what planning in travel and tourism is all about. Three points need to be emphasised:

1 Planning is a process mapping out future decisions or actions in order to achieve desired outcomes in an appropriate way.

2 Therefore, effective planning depends upon the existence of goals, objectives or policies.

3 Planning is an ongoing process; a plan is the outcome of planning at a particular point in time.

The distinction between policy and plans is clear. A destination's policy *may be to develop particular niche-market tourism; therefore, it will* plan *the development of facilities, as well as its marketing and promotion activities, accordingly.*

The planning process

In principle, the planning process should follow a set of stages, as follows:

1 Policy formulation. Selecting tourism as a contributor to broader development.

2 Identification of goals or objectives. Objectives to meet the overall policy.

3 Collection of data relevant to tourism development. This may be **secondary data** or **primary data**.

4 Analysis of data. Data should be analysed according to a number of key issues, including:

- asset evaluation, and whether new investment is required
- market research/analysis
- impact analysis
- the development process: finance, employment, training, marketing, etc.

5 Preparation of plans.

6 Implementation of plans.

7 Monitoring and evaluation of outcomes. Review planning process with respect to original objectives.

The key point to remember is that planning is not a one-off event; it is, or should be, a continual, pro-active process.

The role of planning in tourism development

As noted already, planning is an essential element of tourism development. Poor planning (or a lack of planning) may lead to environmental or social problems, or a destination's loss of appeal to tourists. More specifically, the nature of the tourism industry points to the need for effective planning.

The key things to remember about planning are that:

- It provides a framework for establishing and assessing clear objectives for tourism development.
- It encourages integrated planning and development of tourism – integrating tourism with economic, social and environmental planning.
- It relates tourism development to available resources.
- It provides the framework for cooperative actions and decision-making among all stakeholders.
- It establishes an overall 'design' for a destination.
- It sets yardsticks by which the outcomes of tourism development can be measured and evaluated according to overall objectives.

It is important to remember that plans are just that – plans. It is easy to plan, but it is harder to implement those plans successfully, particularly in a global and dynamic sector such as travel and tourism that is susceptible to the global political economy and unexpected (and all too frequent) external events or crises.

The objectives of planning

The broad objectives of planning in travel and tourism are to optimise developmental benefits and to minimise costs or impacts. Therefore, there are two sets of objectives, namely, developmental objectives and management objectives. Developmental objectives can be categorised under three headings:

1 *Improvement in the economy.* It is probably true to say that the principal developmental benefit of travel and tourism is economic growth.

2 **Community integration.** Tourism development should be integrated into the social and economic life of local communities so that their needs should figure prominently in tourism planning.

3 **Visitor experience.** Planning should focus on developing tourism to meet or exceed tourists' needs and expectations.

The management objective is protection and enhancement of the resource base upon which tourism depends.

Approaches to planning

The way in which planning in travel and tourism is approached also varies. First, planning occurs at different levels in the tourism system:

1 *International level.* You will undoubtedly come across booklets and documents, either in your library or on the Internet, published by organisations such as the World Tourism Organization or the World Travel and Tourism Council. (Other bodies, such as UNEP, also publish documents relating to tourism.) These organisations have no real power or authority – if you read their publications it rapidly becomes evident that they propose only guidelines that may inform tourism planning at the national level.

2 *National level.* National tourism planning sets out the travel and tourism development plans for the country as a whole. However, the detail and extent of national government influence in relevant areas, such as legislation, education and training, infrastructural developments, taxation, marketing and so on varies enormously from one country to the next.

3 *Local/destination level.* At the local level, planning is much more detailed and addresses specific issues such as the nature, scale and number of facilities and attractions, local transport needs, and so on.

Publications by organisations such as the WTO provide useful sets of principles or guidelines with respect to tourism planning and development. However, perhaps their greatest value lies in the case studies that they provide.

Second, planning may be driven by different perspectives or philo-sophies. The contemporary approach is, of course, sustainable tourism development, with planning designed to balance the needs of all stakeholders within environmental constraints, but you need to be aware of other approaches to planning tourism:

1 *'Boosterism':* a simplistic focus on planning tourism to opti-mise short-term benefits. One example is the promotion of mega-events, such as the Olympic Games.

2 *Economic approach:* the principal focus is on economic growth. Planning, development and marketing is designed to optimise economic returns.

3 *Land-use approach:* planning that places the protection of the physical environment at the centre of the tourism develop-ment process.

4 *Community tourism planning:* a 'bottom-up' approach to tourism planning designed to optimise local communities' involvement in and benefit from tourism development. The objec-tives of community-based tourism are to:

- give local communities some control over tourism development
- ensure that local socio-economic needs inform the basic objectives of tourism planning
- give local communities some control over resource use
- optimise local communities' benefits from tourism.

Despite the widespread support for community-based planning, it does not always succeed in practice. It is well worth considering the reasons why community tourism planning often fails.

Who plans for tourism?

The final but, perhaps, most important issue you need to think about is: where does the responsibility for planning travel and tourism lie? In other words, it is easy to describe the planning process, but it is less clear who should devise and implement those plans. In many countries it is the national tourism organisation but elsewhere it may be devolved to local private–public sector partnerships.

The key issue is the balance between public sector (government) involvement in planning and private sector implementation of those plans. Given the explicit link between tourism and regional or national development, it is logical to suggest that governments should take a leading role in planning tourism as they are in a position to:

- set out overall development policy
- establish the contribution of tourism to development
- determine the approach to tourism development
- establish the financial and regulatory framework for tourism development.

However, governments typically adopt a passive approach to involvement in tourism planning, particularly in developed countries, supporting tourism development but not being actively involved in it. Conversely, in less developed countries, governments often take a more active role, usually because the private sector does not possess the expertise or capital to take the lead in developing tourism. However, the extent to which government-led planning is implemented is dependent on the local political economy.

Planning for travel and tourism cannot be divorced from local or national political and economic structures. Frequently, governments or national tourism organisations develop comprehensive tourism development plans, but are unable to implement them because of the economic or political power of local social or business groups.

Taking it **FURTHER**

Given the sectoral diversity of the travel and tourism industry, planning tourism is a complex process. However, in many countries a variety of public sector organisations also have a legitimate interest in tourism planning and development. These may be local government bodies, conservation organisations, national park authorities, and so on, or government departments with responsibilities that embrace tourism, such as rural development agencies, employment or business development agencies or transport ministries. Therefore, the first step in tourism planning may be the development of an organisational map to identify the most significant players in the system.

Typically, exam questions concerned with the topic of tourism planning will focus on either the need for tourism planning or on particular aspects of the planning process, such as its complexity or the variety of possible approaches. In either case, you should have examples of tourism planning (both successful and unsuccessful) to hand so that you will be able to illustrate your answers.

A straightforward question, but one that is quite difficult to answer, might be:

❝Why is it necessary to plan travel and tourism?❞

The fundamental reason for planning tourism is to ensure that it meets its broader developmental objectives. However, a number of more specific reasons exist, often related to the specific characteristics of destinations, the type of tourism/tourists, the local political economy, specific policy objectives or, more generally, the overall complexity of the tourism system and the principal objectives of different players within the system. Therefore, your answer should highlight these reasons, also considering how they might be addressed within the planning process.

Alternatively, you may be asked to consider the issue of who should be responsible for tourism planning:

❝Critically appraise the extent to which governments should take an active role in planning travel and tourism.❞

All governments are, to a greater or lesser extent, involved in planning tourism. However, in developed, market-based economies, government involvement in tourism is much less significant than in less developed countries. Nevertheless, there are significant reasons why all governments should take an active role in planning tourism, whether at the national or local level. Your answer should explore these reasons, focusing in particular on the potential conflict between the multitude of possible players in the planning process.

Textbook guide

17	
tourism and the environment	

Travel and tourism is an environmentally dependent activity. In other words, the environment is the very basis of travel and tourism. As tourists, we seek out different and distinctive environments, and our overall tourism experience very much depends on our interaction with the destination environment. At the same time, however, our activities as tourists (or, indeed, the actions of the tourism industry) may threaten or damage that environment, potentially destroying the very thing that attracted us in the first place. Therefore, understanding the nature and causes of tourism's environmental impacts, and the ways of minimising them, is of fundamental importance to the planning, management and development of travel and tourism.

In most textbooks and articles, the 'environment' is usually taken to mean the physical (natural and man-made) environment, as distinct from the destination's society, economy and culture. However, from a tourist's perspective, the environment comprises not only the physical environment, but also the social, historical, architectural and cultural fabric of the destination, that collectively contribute to its identity and which may be collectively damaged by tourism. Therefore, although the physical and other types of tourism impact are usually studied separately, in reality they cannot be divorced from each other.

Not surprisingly, the study of travel and tourism has long been concerned with tourism's environmental impacts – in fact, it was probably the first hot topic in tourism and, invariably, your course will include a module dealing, in some form or another, with the environmental impacts of tourism. It also features in most general textbooks, while a number of books focus specifically on tourism and the environment. However, perhaps one of the best introductions to the topic remains Alistair Mathieson and Geoff Wall's (1982) now classic book on the subject.

First, a word of warning when studying tourism and the environment. It is all too easy to just list and give examples of the negative and positive impacts on the environment. However, not only is it a complex topic, but it is also better to focus on ways of managing the impacts of travel and tourism. Simply describing them is unlikely to impress your examiner.

The topic is not as straightforward as you might first imagine because:

- It is not always clear whether environmental change has been directly caused by tourism or by other human activities.
- The environmental impacts of tourism may not always be immediate or obvious.
- Tourism development may result in indirect or induced environmental impacts, sometimes in locations other than the destination.
- Frequently, baselines for measuring the environmental consequences of travel and tourism do not exist.

Moreover, it is also important to recognise the extent to which particular environments are perceived differently by different stakeholders. That is, local communities may view their environment as a resource in a very different light from visitors, while visitors themselves may have varying attitudes towards the destination environment, from a place to be exploited to a place to be conserved.

There is, in effect, no single travel and tourism environment in a destination. Different groups of locals or tourists will have different perceptions, needs and expectations and, by implication, there are different ways in which the environment can or should be managed.

It is, of course, necessary to be aware of the positive and negative impacts of travel and tourism on the environment, and these are summarised below. However, it is useful to first consider two issues: the tourism–environment relationship and the factors affecting the level of impacts.

The tourism–environment relationship

Although it has long been recognised that the development of travel and tourism almost inevitably has environmental consequences, it is only since the emergence of mass, international tourism that it has been considered a problem. It has been suggested that there have been four stages in the tourism–environment relationship:

1 *Co-existence:* pre-mass tourism, when tourism had a limited environmental impact.

2 *Conflict:* mass tourism seen as a destroyer of environments.

3 *Idealism:* potential **symbiosis** through the development of alternative, 'green' tourism.

4 *Realism:* different approaches to development that balance the needs of tourists and locals with those of the environment.

Similarly, there are three possible relationships between tourism and the environment, namely, neutrality, conflict or harmony; harmony (or symbiosis) is the ideal, though it is rarely achieved.

Factors affecting the level of impacts

Particular activities or pressures do not always have the same environmental consequences. In other words, the degree or extent to which travel and tourism impacts (or is perceived to impact) positively or negatively on the environment is determined by a variety of factors. These include:

1 The fragility or robustness of the environment: some environments are more physically or ecologically robust than others.

2 The scale and speed of tourism development: slower, planned development may reduce the level of impact.

3 The extent to which tourism development is integrated into the local environment: appropriate development reduces impacts such as **architectural pollution**.

4 The political context of tourism development: weak political systems may 'allow' environmental degradation through inappropriate development.

5 The number of tourists visiting a destination: when the **physical carrying capacity** of a destination is exceeded (see Section 19).

6 The types of tourist and their activities at the destination: different behaviours may impact more or less on fragile environments.

7 The attitudes of local people towards their environment: the environment may be seen as a resource to be exploited, not conserved or protected (or vice versa).

The environmental impacts of tourism

Many books describe in some detail the impacts of tourism on destination environments. These may be both positive and negative. Positive impacts include:

- the creation of protected areas (national parks, wildlife sanctuaries, etc.)
- conservation and improvement of the physical environment (natural and man-made)
- protection and repair of ancient monuments, historic houses, etc.

An important point is that any conservation/protection policy, directly or indirectly motivated by the needs of tourism, must be considered from the local community's perspective. Such 'positive' impacts may disrupt traditional activities and lifestyles.

Not surprisingly, perhaps, greater attention is paid to the negative impacts of travel and tourism.

These impacts include:

1 Depletion of natural resources, particularly water.

2 Physical damage:

- erosion of footpaths, sand dunes and ecologically fragile areas
- damage caused by inappropriate/illegal activities (campfires, illegal parking, etc.)

- disfigurement or damage to historical sites or monuments though graffiti or theft
- infrastructural development on sensitive sites (ski-lifts, etc.).

3 Impacts on wildlife:

- disruption of feeding or migration patterns
- hunting and fishing.

4 Pollution:

- physical pollution (land, sea, air)
- noise pollution
- architectural pollution.

> *Tourism is frequently used as a scapegoat, being blamed for a variety of environmental and other impacts. It is also easy to be subjective or emotional in assessing tourism's impacts. However, not only is it important to remain objective, but you should also consider other factors that may contribute to environmental degradation.*

Managing tourism and the environment

Although it is important to be able to identify and explain the different types of environmental impacts, attention should be focused primarily on the ways and means of managing such impacts. This can be done from a number of perspectives:

1 *Managing physical resources.* The physical resources, natural or man-made, upon which tourism depends can be managed at different levels:

- Land designation: the creation of designated protected areas (e.g. national parks, nature reserves) where the needs of conservation and tourism can be balanced.
- Spatial planning strategies: methods, such as zoning, of matching tourism development and activity to land characteristics.
- Site management techniques: local, site-level techniques, such as the type and location of visitor facilities.

2 *Managing visitors.* The impacts of tourism are, to a great extent, related to tourist behaviour and activity. Therefore, a variety of visitor management techniques may be employed to minimise visitor-induced impacts (see Section 19).

3 *Sustainable tourism development.* Sustainable tourism development attempts to address the needs of all stakeholders in the tourism destination – the physical environment, local communities, the tourism industry and tourists themselves. The objectives of sustainable tourism development are embodied in varying sets of principles which act as a blueprint for tourism development. These have, however, been widely criticised as a 'one-size-fits-all' approach to tourism which does not allow for:

- local attitudes towards resource exploitation
- perceptions of the limits of acceptable change
- local social and economic development needs
- the right of local communities to manage, or have an input into the management of, their own environment.

4 *Regulations/policies.* The environmental impacts of tourism may be managed by regional or national policies, such as environmental action plans or specific programmes such as the European Blue Flag scheme (www.blueflag.org). Tourism development may also be subject to environmental impact assessments.

5 *Systems approach.* Most recently, environmental management systems have been proposed as a means of planning and managing tourism environments. Implicit in these are the concepts of local environmental governance (where local communities are architects of local environmental development) and ecological dynamism, which recognises that all environments are in a continual state of change. Therefore, environmental planning starts not with the needs of tourists or the tourism industry, but with local environmental attitudes and knowledge and local developmental needs.

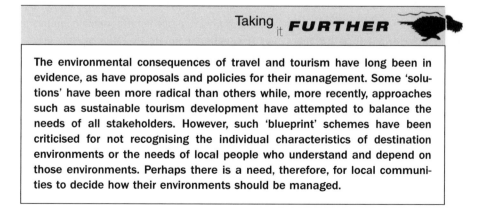

Taking it **FURTHER**

The environmental consequences of travel and tourism have long been in evidence, as have proposals and policies for their management. Some 'solutions' have been more radical than others while, more recently, approaches such as sustainable tourism development have attempted to balance the needs of all stakeholders. However, such 'blueprint' schemes have been criticised for not recognising the individual characteristics of destination environments or the needs of local people who understand and depend on those environments. Perhaps there is a need, therefore, for local communities to decide how their environments should be managed.

Questions on tourism and the environment are unlikely to ask you to simply identify different positive and negative impacts. Rather, you will be asked to consider broader issues related to the topic, such as ways of managing the tourism environment or where the responsibility for environmental management lies. For example, you may be asked:

❝What role can local or national governments play in managing the environmental consequences of tourism development? ❞

There are various causes of the environmental consequences of travel and tourism development, such as the activities/operations of the travel industry or the activities of tourists themselves. Depending on the political economy of the destination, governments may be more or less able to regulate the development of tourism, although there are specific issues, such as aviation policy or the environmental restrictions on resort development, where regulations may be imposed.

Alternatively, a more specific question may ask:

❝Why is it important to consider the environmental consequences of tourism, and potential responses, on a destination-by-destination basis? ❞

All tourism destinations suffer, to a lesser or greater extent, similar categories of environmental impact as a result of tourism development. However, the intensity of those impacts, and how they are perceived, varies enormously according to local environmental attitudes and development needs, as well as the scale/ nature of tourism development and the type/activities of tourists themselves. Therefore, it is not possible to apply a rigid set of principles to managing and developing the tourism environment.

Typically, concern for tourism's impacts focuses on the destination environment. However, you may be asked to:

"Critically appraise the need to consider the direct and indirect environmental impacts of tourism."

Tourism does not occur only in destinations, but also in the generating region and the transit region. Moreover, travel and tourism is a global activity, impacting on the global environment. Therefore, it is important to consider not only direct impacts, whether at a site or regional level, but also the indirect impacts both in the destination and other tourism regions. A local tourism development may, for example, be environmentally sustainable, but the environmental impact of international transport to that destination may be significant. Thus, the total environmental 'cost' may be much higher than that resulting from direct environmental impact in the destination.

Textbook guide

COOPER ET AL. **(2005):** *Chapter 6*
HOLDEN **(2000)**
HOLLOWAY **(2002):** *Chapter 17*
MATHIESON AND WALL **(1982):** *Chapters 2 and 4*
PENDER AND SHARPLEY **(2005):** *Chapter 18*
SHARPLEY **(2002):** *Chapter 11*

18	
tourism, society and culture	

Travel and tourism is a social phenomenon. Therefore, it inevitably lends itself to sociological analysis and some of the key thinkers in tourism, such as Erik Cohen and John Urry, are themselves sociologists. Anthropologists have, likewise, long turned their attention to tourism, a classic, edited book being Valene Smith's *Hosts and Guests: The Anthropology of Tourism*, first published in 1977. More recently, tourism has also found its way onto the cultural studies agenda and, overall, there is a rich, varied and sometimes complex literature on the socio-cultural aspects of tourism. However, unless you have a specific interest in exploring tourism in some depth from a sociological or cultural perspective, a simpler analysis of the relationship between tourism, society and culture will suffice.

As fascinating, and sometimes emotive, as the socio-cultural study of travel and tourism is, it is important to bear in mind why we study it. Certainly, there is much to learn from tourism about social behaviour, consumer culture, intercultural exchange and so on but, from a travel and tourism perspective, the purpose is simply to understand, and better manage, the tourist.

There is, essentially, a two-way relationship between the tourist and the society/cultures which both generate and receive tourists. On the one hand, tourists are influenced by their home society and culture; the motivation to participate in tourism in the first place is largely determined by society, while tourist behaviour – the needs, expectations, perceptions and actual consumer behaviour of tourists, is socially and culturally defined. Often overlooked, but nevertheless also important, is the impact of destination societies on tourists. That is, tourists' attitudes, beliefs and cultural behaviour may be transformed by their socio-cultural experiences in destinations.

On the other hand, of course, tourists impact both negatively and positively upon destination societies. Some of the earliest work in this area explored the social impacts and it remains an area of significant concern within tourism studies, particularly in the context of tourism-related prostitution and child sex. Moreover, much of the work of the London-based pressure group Tourism Concern addresses these and other social issues related to tourism development – it is well worth accessing their website (www.tourismconcern.org.uk) in order to see the variety of issues or problems brought about by tourism.

There are, then, three key issues to focus on when looking at tourism, society and culture:

1 Social influences on tourism.

2 The tourist–host relationship.

3 Socio-cultural impacts of tourism.

Social influences on tourism

Travel and tourism is a product of modern society; that is, modern society not only provides the means to be a tourist (time, income, transport, etc.), but also the motivation to participate in tourism. The influence of society on tourist behaviour is manifested in a number of ways, most of which are explored in the context of tourism demand and motivation (see Sections 3 and 4). These can be summarised as follows:

1 *Tourist typologies.* The work of Erik Cohen, for example, is based upon a tourist's relationship with his/her home society and the consequential desire to seek the familiar or the unfamiliar/novel.

2 *Tourist motivation.* A number of extrinsic socio-cultural factors influence tourist motivation. These include family influences, **reference groups**, social class/background and wider cultural influences. The work–tourism relationship is also a significant factor in determining both the motivation for tourism and tourist behaviour.

3 *Modern society.* Modern society allegedly creates a sense of alienation/anomie; that is, people suffer a sense of meaningless/'placelessness'. This can be felt in:

- alienation at work: separation from the outcome/product of work
- alienation from community: mobility and information technology have reduced face-to-face communication and a sense of community
- alienation from nature: urban living separates people from nature and the natural world.

As a result of the alleged alienation tourists suffer in modern societies, they are motivated to seek authenticity (a sense of meaning or reality) through tourism. This may be found in authentic places (usually associated with less developed or pre-modern societies) and/or authentic forms of travel (niche travel experiences, usually overland). Authenticity has, therefore, become a powerful marketing tool in travel and tourism.

It is also important to be aware of the link between tourism and postmodern culture. At one level, this represents a way of describing particular types of tourism or tourist attractions which reflect the characteristics of postmodernity. More specifically, however, the identification of the self through consumption (or consumer culture) is considered to be a defining feature of postmodernity. Therefore, the way in which tourism is consumed may be influenced by postmodern consumer culture (see Sharpley, 2003, Chapters 3 and 6).

Travel and tourism has always been a status symbol. From a consumer culture perspective, it remains a powerful means of creating self-identity.

In effect, any one type or form of tourism may be consumed in a number of different ways by different tourists, depending on what they hope to gain from the experience. There are four categories of tourism consumption that are worth considering:

1 *Consuming as experience.* The consumption of tourism is influenced by the meaning attached to tourism in the tourist's own society.

2 *Consuming as play.* Tourism is used a means of interacting (playing) with other tourists.

3 *Consuming as integration.* This is the attempt to integrate oneself into the destination or the tourism activity.

4 *Consuming as classification.* Consuming to create status or self-identity.

The tourist–host relationship

Tourists inevitably come into contact with local people at the destination: this contact is referred to as the tourist–host encounter or tourist–host relationship. The nature of this relationship may determine the extent to which negative social impacts are experienced in the destination and, therefore, understanding the processes involved in tourist–host encounters/relationships may help to minimise such impacts.

Although local communities are often referred to as 'hosts' and tourists as 'guests', the implied balance in their relationship does not usually exist in practice – the nature of tourist–host encounters (brief, transitory and often based on economic exchange) suggests a lack of balance and potential conflict.

There are two concepts that you need to be aware of when looking at the tourist–host relationship:

1 *The tourist area life cycle* (TALC). As destinations pass through different stages of the life cycle, local people's per-ceptions of tourists may vary from initial welcome and open-ness to eventual distrust and antagonism. See also Section 15.

2 *The 'Irridex'*. Similar to the TALC, it is suggested that local com-munities progress through four stages as tourism develops: euphoria, apathy, irritation and antagonism.

A number of studies have been undertaken into host attitudes towards tourists. Not surprisingly, perhaps, local people feel more positive about tourists the more they are dependent upon tourism as a source of income.

The socio-cultural impacts of tourism

Inevitably, the development of tourism impacts upon local communities in destination areas. Social impacts may be described (somewhat simplistically) as those that are more immediate and visible, whereas cultural impacts are changes that occur over a longer period of time.

Tourism is often blamed for the socio-cultural impacts or changes that occur among destination communities. However, it is important to consider other factors either within the community or more generally through the process of globalisation that may contribute to such impacts.

Some socio-cultural impacts may be positive. As an agent of develop-ment, tourism may contribute to higher incomes, greater employment opportunities, improved education and healthcare facilities, infrastruc-tural developments, and an overall improvement in local communities' quality of life. However, more often than not attention is focused on the so-called 'negative' social and cultural impacts of tourism. The extent to which these may be felt are dependent upon the:

- types or numbers of tourists
- size and development of the tourism industry
- relative importance of the tourism industry
- pace of tourism development.

Most textbooks describe in some detail the negative social impacts or consequences of tourism. Generally, these may be in the form of social or community restructuring, as people move to resort areas on the coast to find employment. This rural–urban migration pattern often results in a population imbalance in rural areas and the polarisation of local societies between younger, more affluent groups and the older, perhaps more traditional generations.

However, the physical presence of tourists, their behaviour and their interaction with local people impacts upon local communities in a variety of ways. Some of these may be immediate, such as inappropriate behaviour, displays of conspicuous consumption or simply the inconvenience caused by large numbers of holidaymakers, causing annoyance or resentment among the local population. Other categories of impact which you need to be aware of include:

- the demonstration effect
- crime
- language
- religion
- sex/prostitution.

Over time, the culture of host societies may change and adapt either directly or indirectly as a result of tourism. Attention is usually paid in particular to the way in which cultural forms, such as arts and crafts or carnivals, festivals and religious events become adapted, trivialised and packaged for consumption by tourists. For example, many art forms become mass-produced as souvenirs (i.e. 'airport art') while, frequently, cultural rituals are transformed and staged for tourists, becoming devoid of all meaning to the participants. This process is referred to as **commodification**.

Tourism also contributes to broader, deeper cultural transformations in destination societies. These are changes that occur in a society's values, moral codes, behavioural modes and identifying characteristics, such as dress and language. Such changes may occur as a result of globalisation and other factors, but it is generally accepted that tourism can accelerate this process, largely through what is known as **acculturation**.

Taking it *FURTHER*

The socio-cultural study of tourism explores the phenomenon from two perspectives: socio-cultural influences on tourism and the impacts of tourism on the destination society and culture. Generally, these are seen as separate issues. That is, an increasing number of books and articles consider tourism as a cultural phenomonen, with entire series of books dedicated to the issue, while, more often than not, the study of social impacts is relegated to chapters in general texts. However, there is potentially much to learn by combining both perspectives. For example, what can the different forms of tourism consumption tell us about managing tourism's social impacts? Or, are tourism's impacts a manifestation of cultural globalisation?

As travel and tourism is a social phenomenon, questions relating to the socio-cultural study of tourism may, in principle, address virtually any aspect of the subject. However, you are most likely to be set questions that explore one or both of the two main perspectives that we have identified in this section. Regarding socio-cultural influences on tourism, there is an evident link with tourism demand and motivation and questions may, in fact, focus more specifically on those topics. However, you may be asked about the link between tourism and consumer culture. For example:

" Consider the statement that 'tourism is consumed primarily as a means of creating self-identity'. "

There is no doubt that tourism has always been a status symbol. However, as consumer culture becomes increasingly dominant in modern (or postmodern) society, tourism may be consumed in a variety of different ways. Therefore, your answer should: first, review the social and cultural influences on tourism demand, suggesting that the entire process is framed within a consumer culture context; and second, explore why consumer culture is an important consideration, followed by an examination of the different modes of consumption, ideally relating them to a particular type of tourism.

Undoubtedly, questions will focus on some aspect of the socio-cultural impacts of tourism. It is unlikely that you will be simply asked to describe these impacts (and doing so in any question is unlikely to impress your examiner); rather, you may be asked about the process, such as:

> **"Consider the extent to which the social impacts of tourism are dependent upon the relative difference between tourists and host communities. "**

Many texts describe the social impacts of tourism, yet different destinations will experience them to varying extents. You should point out, however, that all destinations will suffer (or benefit from, in the case of positive impacts) some degree of social impact – the challenge is to optimise the positive impacts and minimise the negative impacts. At the same time, all societies are dynamic and, therefore, identifying specific tourism-related impacts may be difficult. Nevertheless, a variety of factors determine the intensity of social impacts and, through an understanding of these, tourism may be developed in such a manner as to reduce its negative impacts on the destination society and culture.

An alternative question might be:

> **"Are tourist–host encounters inevitably imbalanced? "**

This question may be addressed in a number of ways. At a more basic level, the characteristics of tourist–host encounters point to imbalance, but you could also explore concepts such as social-exchange theory as a means of analysing the relationship between tourists and local people. At the same time, aspects of tourist motivation, as well as the concept of dependency theory, are also relevant but, collectively, they suggest that tourist–host encounters are not usually characterised by balance or equality.

Textbook guide

COOPER ET AL. **(2005):** *Chapter 7*
HOLLOWAY **(2002):** *Chapter 17*
MATHIESON AND WALL **(1982):** *Chapter 5*
SHARPLEY **(2002):** *Chapter 20*
SHARPLEY **(2003):** *Chapters 9 and 10*

19	
visitor management	

All tourists and visitors, knowingly or unknowingly, have impacts on tourism destinations and attractions. Sometimes, such impacts are avoidable, such as the dropping of litter or illegal parking of cars on grass verges; more often, however, the impacts of tourism result simply from the sheer volume of tourists. Either way, however, a problem that has long faced the travel and tourism sector is the need to allow access to sites and attractions but, at the same time, find ways and means of protecting those sites and attractions so that tourists do not, in effect, destroy what they have come to see.

In response to this problem, the practice of visitor management has evolved as a means of balancing the needs of tourists, the local community, the place and any other stakeholders in destination areas. Its roots lie in outdoor recreation management, where there has long been a need to manage the activities of visitors to protect fragile environments, but there are evident applications to travel and tourism. Not only is it implicit in the concept (and running theme) of sustainable tourism, but tourists need to be managed in both rural and urban environments, as well as at specific sites and attractions (see Section 9).

Visitor management is, implicitly, a reactive process; a response to the pressures and impacts of tourists at sites and attractions. However, it is also useful to think of it as part of the tourism planning process. Effective design, appropriate facilities and so on may avoid or prevent many of the problems that visitor management is designed to address.

Visitor management is, then, an important part of travel and tourism planning and management although, rather curiously, it is not often considered in detail on travel and tourism courses. You will find that most textbooks mention it in passing but if you are able to use your knowledge of it in relevant assignments and questions, you will undoubtedly add depth to your work.

It is well worth familiarising yourself with two or three examples of tourism sites/ attractions where effective visitor management has been implemented. A number of books provide examples, but it is better to use places that are known to you personally.

The study of visitor management is relatively simple; you need to be aware of the different approaches to, and application of, visitor management techniques, as well as being able to appraise the relative merits of each. An important point to remember, however, is that visitor management is, in a sense, a necessary evil. That is, tourists enjoy the freedom and spontaneity that being on holiday affords them and, to an extent, visitor management may impose some restriction on that freedom. Therefore, visitor management should, ideally:

- be unobtrusive
- be non-regulatory
- enhance the visitor experience.

As a starting point, it is useful to consider the concept of carrying capacity. Based on the idea that all sites, attractions or destinations have a finite capacity beyond which the environment, the life of local communities and the enjoyment of visitors may be impaired, four types of carrying capacity may be considered:

1 *Physical carrying capacity:* usually applicable to enclosed spaces, this is the physical limit to the number of people a site can accommodate.

2 *Ecological carrying capacity:* beyond which the ecology of the site is impaired.

3 *Social carrying capacity:* beyond which the socio-cultural life of local communities is disrupted.

4 *Psychological carrying capacity:* the level of congestion that will be tolerated by tourists before their enjoyment is spoilt.

The concept of carrying capacity remains debatable, mainly because many measurements are based on value judgements. Nevertheless, it provides a framework for considering when visitor management may be necessary.

Approaches to visitor management

Typically, visitor management techniques are categorised as hard measures (extensive and permanent restrictions on visitors' activities) or soft measures, such as interpretation or marketing. An alternative and, perhaps, clearer categorisation identifies three levels of visitor management according to the degree of regulation involved:

1 *Influencing visitor behaviour.* This is designed to raise visitors' awareness of the impacts of their behaviour and to encourage them to alter it. Techniques include:

- codes of conduct
- marketing (and de-marketing), information provision, interpretation
- 'on-the-ground' advice (e.g. rangers).

2 *Redistributing demand.* This attempts to redistribute demand from fragile to more robust sites or attractions. Techniques include:

- marketing, signage: e.g. promoting other, less visited areas, or creating 'tourist routes'
- zoning: the division of areas according to desired level or type of use.

3 *Rationing demand.* This is the most regulatory/restrictive level, with techniques designed to limit demand at any one time. Techniques include:

- time-tickets
- limited car parking
- permits/advance booking
- guided tours
- pricing
- denying access.

While the first two categories of visitor management are most applicable to open areas or sites, rationing demand techniques are most applicable to enclosed sites or attractions. These may be nature reserves, gardens or other fragile or protected outdoor sites, as well as museums, historic houses and so on.

Visitor management models

A number of different models of visitor management have been implemented around the world, though largely in the context of natural areas, national parks and wilderness areas. These include:

1 *Recreation opportunity spectrum.* Threshold levels of use are determined in the planning and management of sites.

2 *Carrying capacity model.* Imposes a maximum number of visitors allowed into the site at any one time.

3 *Limits of acceptable change.* Sets limits on how much change to the site/attraction is acceptable.

Taking it **FURTHER**

As travel and tourism continues to increase in volume, and as more and more tourists travel to more distant, exotic locations, visitor management will become a more pressing issue for many places, sites and attractions. Although the least regulatory, soft methods are the most desirable, it is likely that rationing demand will become more extensive. Should it also be the case, though, that visitors should pay for the upkeep of sites and attractions? That is, should pricing be used, where appropriate, both to ration demand and to fulfil the 'polluter pays' principle?

Questions on visitor management almost invariably focus on the applicability of different types of management to different contexts. Therefore, you should always have examples at hand to bring your answers to life. A typical, general question would be:

"Critically appraise the applicability of different visitor management techniques to different contexts."

Justifying the need for visitor management, you would explore the different levels and types of visitor management, drawing on examples to demonstrate their effectiveness. The overall theme would be that the most desirable form of visitor management is the least regulatory although, in some circumstances, denying access is the only solution.

Recognising that the origins of visitor management techniques lie in the planning and management of outdoor recreation, another question might be:

"How necessary or applicable are visitor management techniques to tourism resort areas?"

Again drawing on examples, answers should first identify the 'typical' problems that resort areas face before going on to explore the range of techniques that may be utilised to manage visitors in resort areas.

Textbook guide

PAGE (2003): *Chapter 12*
SHACKLEY (2001): *Chapters 2 to 5*

20	
urban tourism	

Throughout history, towns and cities have been a focus of tourist activity, providing accommodation, entertainment and other facilities for visitors. The structure of the **Grand Tour**, for example, was determined to a great extent by the location of Europe's culturally significant cities, while other towns and cities of historical or cultural importance have long attracted visitors. However, although much of the world's tourism activity occurs in urban settings, from major capital cities to coastal resorts, it is only recently that urban tourism has been identified as a significant sector of tourism worthy of academic attention. There are two main reasons for this:

1 Since the early 1980s, the potential contribution of tourism to urban regeneration, particularly in towns and cities not traditionally associated with tourism, has become more widely recognised. Tourism is now a virtually ubiquitous element of urban regeneration policy.

2 Transformations in the demand for travel and tourism, influenced particularly by the expansion of low cost, no-frills

flights, have put many more towns and cities on the tourism map, significantly increasing competition within the urban tourism sector.

The increasing academic interest in the broad area of urban tourism is, of course, reflected in the growing number of books on the subject. What you will find, however, is that they vary in focus and content. Some, for example, deal with issues related to image and marketing, others are concerned specifically with historic places, while yet others take a more structured approach to the management of urban tourism in general.

> *Common to the study of other areas within travel and tourism, the perspective taken on urban tourism will very much depend on the interest and disciplinary background of your lecturer. Nevertheless, you should look at one or two of the key texts, particularly Law (2002) and Page and Hall (2003),to identify the main issues relevant to urban tourism.*

Despite this diversity, there are a number of core themes relevant to urban tourism of which you need to be aware. However, first of all it is worth thinking about what urban tourism actually is. In other words, you could quite rightly suggest that most tourism, other than that which occurs in natural, rural or wilderness areas, is urban as it takes place in urban areas! This generalisation points to the difficulty in defining or categorising urban tourism. For example, tourist towns and cities may be categorised by demand and supply, such as tourist cities, shopping cities, culture cities or historic cities, although, in reality, many cities are a combination of all of these (and people may visit cities for a variety of reasons). Perhaps a more useful categorisation is:

1 *Resort cities:* those built for tourism as a primary function.

2 *Tourist-historic cities:* where a city's heritage becomes the tourism attraction.

3 *Converted cities:* where a change of function has occurred.

The roles of towns and cities may also vary. Some are attractions in their own right, some are 'gateway' cities, and some provide a focus for regional tourism. Therefore, not only is there, in effect, no single or definable 'urban tourism', but also the issues and challenges facing the development of urban tourism are unique to each town/city context.

> *Although urban tourism is a diverse phenomenon, the nature and function of tourism in an urban setting will be determined by the nature of that urban setting. In tourism studies, that urban setting is typically a 'converted' city that has used tourism, in some form or another, for the purpose of economic and social regeneration.*

As towns and cities are destinations, a number of the key themes in urban tourism are common to tourism as a whole; that is, the city, in a sense, provides a context or focus for the study of tourism (and it is no coincidence that much of the urban tourism literature is case-study based). Themes that you will need to address are demand for urban tourism, supply of urban tourism, urban regeneration, and urban tourism and place marketing.

Demand for urban tourism

It is important to understand the demand for urban tourism – who visits towns and cities, what motivates them to go there, what they do when they get there – in order to be better able to meet their needs as tourists. However, analysing the demand for urban tourism is problematic. That is, towns and cities are multifunctional and tourists may visit for a variety of reasons. The principal purpose may not even be tourism. At the same time, many facilities and attractions may be used by residents or non-residents working in the city. Thus, assessing the demand for urban tourism is a difficult, if not impossible task, although one useful way of segmenting demand is by resident–non-resident and intentional–incidental use of tourism facilities.

Supply of urban tourism

The supply of urban tourism refers to the bundle of attractions and facilities that comprise a town or city's overall tourism product. This, of course, varies enormously from one place to another and, as with the demand for urban tourism, assessing supply is complicated by the fact that some facilities are provided for residents as well as tourists – in fact, their primary purpose is as a service for residents (e.g. shops). However, it has been suggested that the supply of urban tourism can be categorised as follows:

1 Primary elements:

- activity place: cultural facilities, sports facilities, amusement facilities
- leisure setting: physical characteristics, socio-cultural characteristics.

2 Secondary elements:

- hotel and catering facilities
- markets
- shopping facilities.

3 Additional elements:

- accessibility, parking facilities
- tourist facilities: information services, etc.

Evidently, however, hotels or shopping facilities could be primary elements, while primary elements could also be secondary.

The complexity of developing a picture of a city's tourism supply can easily be demonstrated by listing all the attractions/facilities in a city known to you according to the above classification.

Tourism and urban regeneration

The principal purpose of developing urban tourism is the socio-economic regeneration of urban spaces, such as dockland areas or inner cities, thereby stimulating economic growth, inward investment, infra-structural improvements, and so on. A variety of strategies may be employed, depending upon the attributes of different cities:

- event-led strategies (e.g. Olympic Games)
- attraction-led strategies (creating a core, critical mass of attractions)
- business-led strategies (e.g. conference tourism)
- culture strategies (promoting heritage or contemporary culture)
- leisure-activity strategies (e.g. shopping, cinema, theatre, etc.).

However, although there are many commonly cited examples of success stories, such as Barcelona, you need to be aware of a number of problems or challenges associated with the development of tourism as a vehicle for urban regeneration:

1 *Social exclusion.* New developments may be socially exclusive, bringing benefits to those who least need them.

2 *Contestation of space.* There may be different opinions over how urban space should be developed.

3 *Resource allocation.* Resources allocated to tourism attractions may be better allocated to more socially worthwhile causes.

4 *Community involvement.* A lack of community involvement may lead to resentment.

5 *Political environment.* Objectives may be driven by broader political motives rather than by local developmental needs.

Urban tourism and place marketing

It has become increasingly important for tourist towns and cities to market themselves effectively – **place marketing** has evolved as a form of marketing designed to promote the town/city as a product to the tourist. Part of this process is the development of an image or brand for which the city becomes known and sought after. However, as more and more towns and cities strive to become destinations, replicating development models, problems have evolved:

- Many urban destinations are the 'same' (e.g. indistinguishable docklands developments).
- Marketing campaigns to promote difference are themselves homogeneous.
- Faced with greater competition, many cities have joined together in marketing campaigns.

It is, therefore, becoming increasingly difficult for cities to market themselves in a crowded 'place market'.

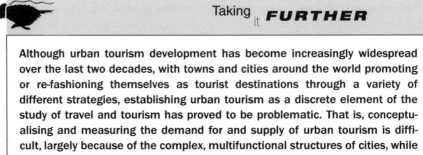

Taking it *FURTHER*

Although urban tourism development has become increasingly widespread over the last two decades, with towns and cities around the world promoting or re-fashioning themselves as tourist destinations through a variety of different strategies, establishing urban tourism as a discrete element of the study of travel and tourism has proved to be problematic. That is, conceptualising and measuring the demand for and supply of urban tourism is difficult, largely because of the complex, multifunctional structures of cities, while the diversity of towns and cities, their tourism product and the strategies they employ to develop tourism, means that it is difficult to form general models of urban tourism development. Therefore, it may be better to think in terms of subcategories of urban tourism rather than adopting an overarching approach to the subject.

There are many examples of urban tourism development in practice. You should familiarise yourself with a number of these, from historic cities to those, such as Sydney or Barcelona, that have hosted the Olympics, to use as examples for exam questions. At the same time, however, you should be aware of some of the key debates within the topic of urban tourism, as you may be asked a simple question such as:

"Is there an 'urban tourist'?"

Much tourism occurs in towns and cities and, therefore, an urban tourist may simply be a tourist in an urban setting. However, studies of the demand for urban tourism demonstrate that even just identifying the urban tourist is difficult, while measuring and categorising demand is even harder. Highlighting the diversity and complexity of the demand for urban tourism, your answer should relate this to the character of towns and cities as multifunctional places, concluding that there is probably not an 'urban tourist'.

The key theme in urban tourism is regeneration and a high-profile strategy is the hosting of a mega-event. Therefore, a possible question would be:

"Critically appraise the contribution of mega-events to urban regeneration?"

There are undoubtedly success stories, such as the continuing tourist development of Barcelona after the Olympics. Equally, there are many examples where successful regeneration has not followed such events. Drawing on examples, your answer should explore the variety of strategies for urban regeneration through tourism, pointing to the need to develop a range of attractions that build upon the initial, though often short-lived benefits of the mega-event.

A fundamental element of successful urban tourism development is marketing, so a possible question would be:

"Consider the importance of developing a brand in place marketing."

Highlighting the increasing competition within the urban tourism market and the factors that are driving it, your answer should demonstrate the need for and importance of place marketing. However, it is not enough to simply promote the particular attractions or features of a place. As tourists face greater choice through improved transport links and the increased supply of urban tourism opportunities, there is a need for cities to create distinctiveness through the development of an image or brand.

Textbook guide

LAW (2002)
PAGE (1995): *Chapters 1 to 3*
PAGE AND HALL (2003): *Chapters 1, 4, 5, 7 and 8*
PENDER AND SHARPLEY (2005): *Chapter 11*
SHAW AND WILLIAMS (2002): *Chapter 10*

21	
rural tourism	

Rural areas have attracted tourists for well over two hundred years and, nowadays, rural tourism is a significant sector of the overall tourism market in many countries – over a quarter of all Europeans, for example, spend their main holiday in the countryside. However, as rural tourism has become increasingly popular, the number of activities in which tourists participate has also grown, putting ever greater pressure on the rural resource base. At the same time, the economic and social structure of the countryside has been transformed; income and employment in the agricultural sector has declined dramatically and, as a result, tourism has become a favoured means of regenerating the rural economy.

There are, therefore, two distinct areas of interest within the study of rural tourism – the extent to which either of these are covered on your course will very much depend upon where rural tourism fits into your curriculum and the approach adopted by your lecturer (though, ideally, you should have an understanding of both areas). On the one hand, your course may focus on the management of the countryside as a resource for tourism, exploring how the various demands on the countryside can be effectively balanced and managed. On the other hand, a developmental perspective concentrates on how tourism can contribute to the social and economic regeneration of rural areas.

You will find that the books you use variously refer to 'tourism', 'leisure' or 'recreation' (or a combination of these) to describe the activity of visitors to the countryside/rural areas. For the sake of simplicity, it is useful to think of all visitors as tourists – however defined, the challenges of managing visitors and of optimising the developmental opportunities afforded by rural tourism are the same.

Irrespective of the focus adopted by your course, however, a number of running themes are relevant to the study of rural tourism. The concept of sustainable tourism development is synonymous with rural tourism, while authenticity is a key issue in terms of rural tourism experiences.

The role of the tourism industry is also important while, more recently, increasing attention has been paid to the governance of the countryside.

As a starting point, there are two interrelated themes that provide the foundation for the study of rural tourism.

The meaning of 'rural'

Academics have long debated (and continue to debate) the meaning of rural or countryside in order to be able to define or identify rural tourism/tourists. In fact, the study of rural tourism often starts by asking if there is such a thing as rural tourism! A key article by Bernard Lane, 'What is rural tourism?' (Bramwell and Lane, 1994), provides a baseline for the debate. There are two ways of considering the issue – tangible and intangible characteristics of the countryside.

Tangible characteristics of the countryside

Simplistically, the countryside may be thought of as areas lying beyond major towns and cities (i.e. 'rural' as opposed to 'urban'). However, this cannot account for the enormous diversity of rural areas and so three characteristics can be used to identify places as rural:

- population density/settlement size
- land use and economy
- social structures.

An important concept to grasp is that of an **urban–rural continuum**. That is, areas become progressively more rural the more distant they lie from centres of population. Consequently, the nature of tourism demand may vary along this continuum while, more generally, the concept suggests that there is no single 'rural' and, hence, no single rural tourism.

Much of the management and promotion of the countryside as a resource for tourism is based upon a number of assumptions about the attraction of the countryside to tourists. Therefore, the concept of the urban–rural continuum is useful in exploring and understanding the true nature of rural tourism.

Intangible characteristics of the countryside

In addition to its tangible characteristics, the countryside has a deeper, cultural meaning or significance to visitors who, predominantly, live and work in urban environments. This meaning varies from one society or country to the next but, essentially, it suggests that tourists visit the countryside for reasons other than going to particular places or participating in particular activities. In short, visiting rural areas provides the opportunity for 'authentic' experiences associated with rural, or non-urban, environments. Frequently, however, this imagined or mythical countryside (images of which are reinforced in brochures or promotional material) does not exist in reality.

The demand for rural tourism

In addition to the 'meaning of rural' debate, it is also important to recognise the key issues related to the demand for rural tourism. It is generally accepted that significant numbers of people participate in rural tourism, yet there remains little consensus as to who or what is a 'rural tourist', or even if it is possible to refer to rural tourism as a separate, identifiable sector of the overall tourism market.

Typically, the demand for rural tourism is considered from a variety of perspectives:

1 *Volume.* This is measured in terms of tourists (i.e. overnight stayers) and day-visitors to areas/places defined as rural.

2 *Characteristics of demand.* Rural tourists are often considered to be more affluent, better educated and representative of the **new tourist**, although surveys show that all socio-economic groups visit the countryside.

3 *Activities.* Visitors to the countryside participate in an enormous variety of activities, some of which are more 'traditional' pursuits, such as hiking, horse-riding or fishing, and others which are not rural in character but depend upon the rural environment.

4 *Motivation.* It is widely assumed that tourists visit the countryside primarily to experience its intrinsic qualities (i.e. 'rurality'). Although surveys have shown this to be the case, more recent research has also shown that, for significant numbers of visitors, it is the opportunity to participate in specific activities (i.e. the intrinsic appeal of the countryside is secondary).

While it is possible to quantify rural tourism in terms of the numbers of visitors to rural areas, it is not realistic to refer to them collectively as rural tourists. Rather, rural tourism is, simply, tourism that occurs in rural areas and it is more useful to distinguish different groups by their activities.

As suggested above, beyond these two underlying themes the study of rural tourism typically follows one or both of two perspectives, namely, managing the countryside resource and planning tourism's role in the socio-economic regeneration of rural areas. These are, of course, related and, ideally, you should have an understanding of both.

Managing the rural resource

There are two key characteristics of the countryside:

1 It is not natural. That is, most rural areas have, to a lesser or greater extent, been influenced or transformed by human intervention.

2 In many countries, it is a multi-purpose resource. That is, a number of different uses/demands (including tourism) compete for a share of the countryside and, as the socio-economic structure of the countryside continues to change, so too does the intensity of different demands.

Managing the countryside, therefore, is concerned in general with balancing demands on the rural resource and, in particular, on managing its use for tourism. Regarding the latter, the principal focus is upon balancing the needs of tourists, the rural tourism industry and the rural resource base. There are four areas that you should familiarise yourself with:

1 *Access issues.* Rural tourism depends upon sufficient and suitable access to the countryside, but this needs to be balanced with patterns of ownership and other legitimate activities.

2 *Land management issues.* A variety of techniques, particularly land designation (e.g. national parks) are employed to balance the different demands on particular areas of the countryside.

3 *Visitor management issues.* As with other tourism places/ spaces, visitor management techniques commonly play an important role in the effective management of rural tourism destinations.

4 *Transport issues.* Sustainable transport policies (for trans-port both to and within the countryside) has become an increasingly important countryside management concern.

Tourism and rural development

Tourism is widely seen as an effective means of stimulating economic and social regeneration in rural areas. Key to this process is the establishment and development of a thriving tourism industry in rural areas in order to provide opportunities for income and employment. A number of contemporary issues deserve attention in this context:

1 *Farm tourism and farm diversification.* Diversification into tourism is widely promoted as a way of meeting the economic challenges faced by the farming sector.

2 *Partnerships, networks and cooperation.* The development of partnerships, networks and **clusters** is seen as a vital ingre-dient of rural tourism development, as is community involvement in tourism.

3 *Marketing.* Key to the success of rural tourism are effective marketing processes and strategies.

4 *Rural tourism planning and development models.* A systems approach to developing rural tourism is seen as the most appropriate means of meeting broader developmental objectives (see Section 17).

Within this theme of rural tourism and development, it is also important to consider the issue of governance and rural tourism policy. The extent to which policies for the development of tourism in the countryside are integrated into broader rural development policy varies from one country to another, but relevant factors include:

- the organisational structure of rural tourism policy
- the dominant 'ideologies' in rural development policy (conservation vs development).

In any rural context, there exists an enormous variety of organisations with a valid contribution to make to rural development policy in general, and rural tourism in particular. These include public sector agencies, conservation bodies, the private sector and voluntary organisations. To demonstrate the complexity of rural governance, it is well worth compiling a list of all such organisations in an area of your choice.

Taking it FURTHER

Rural tourism has attracted ever-increasing academic attention over recent years. However, this attention has been, to a great extent, focused on rural tourism itself; looking at definitional issues, land and access management challenges, and rural tourism business development, rather than at the broader rural context within which tourism is developed. There is a need, therefore, to adopt a new perspective that explores more fully the relationship between the development of tourism and the rural political economy within which it occurs. In particular, it should be asked whether rural tourism should come to occupy a position in rural development policy alongside more traditional concerns, such as agriculture and forestry.

As with most areas within the study of travel and tourism, the questions you are likely to be asked relating to rural tourism will reflect the overall focus of the module and the particular interests of your lecturer. Thus, if your module has looked at managing tourism in the countryside, you may be asked questions regarding access to the countryside, visitor management or the challenges facing national parks. Conversely, the development perspective may be manifested in questions relating to tourism development models. However, it is likely that you will be asked a question that explores the meaning of rural tourism, such as:

" Does the rural tourist exist? "

It has long been assumed that rural tourism is a separate, identifiable sector of the overall tourism market that can be related, in terms of motivation and demand, to the intrinsic characteristics of the countryside. However, not only is there no single 'countryside', but rural areas are undergoing a fundamental transformation (in a sense, becoming less rural). Moreover, visitors to the countryside participate in a wide variety of activities that are not necessarily rural in nature.

Therefore, your answer should explore the contemporary demand for tourism in rural areas within the context of a changing rural environment, concluding that visitors to the countryside should be classified by activity rather than place.

Alternatively, events such as the foot-and-mouth outbreak in the UK have highlighted the lack of connectivity between rural tourism and rural development policy. Therefore, you may be asked to:

“ Critically appraise the extent to which rural tourism should be an integral element of national rural development policy. ”

Tourism is widely seen as an effective means of meeting the socio-economic challenges faced by many rural areas. However, in common with tourism as a whole, the rural tourism industry is diverse, fragmented and difficult to control. At the same time, there are many rural organisations which have a direct or indirect interest in tourism, yet rarely work together. Identifying the potential contribution of tourism to rural development, your answer should highlight the need for a collective approach to developing rural tourism, particularly one which may compete with other powerful interests in the countryside.

Textbook guide

BRAMWELL AND LANE **(1994)**
BUTLER, HALL AND JENKINS **(1998)**
PAGE AND GETZ **(1997)**
ROBERTS AND HALL **(2001)**
SHARPLEY AND SHARPLEY **(1997)**
SHAW AND WILLIAMS **(2002):** *Chapter 11*

22	
contemporary issues in travel and tourism	

Throughout this Companion, it has been suggested that you should try to keep up to date with changes, events, or contemporary issues that occur within the 'real world' of travel and tourism. Simply by registering with one of the online travel and tourism news services, such as travel-mole.com or eturbonews.com, you can receive daily bulletins about international travel and tourism, although just regularly reading newspapers, particularly the travel sections, can also provide you with much valuable information. There are two reasons why you should do this:

1 Travel and tourism is a dynamic industry. There are always new developments, new challenges and new issues and, as a student of travel and tourism, it is important to keep abreast of these.

2 Familiarising yourself with the travel industry, with particular destinations and so on will provide you with a wealth of knowledge that you can draw upon to illustrate or to give an extra dimension to your assignments or exam questions.

Strictly speaking, 'contemporary issues' is not part of the core travel and tourism curriculum, although some courses do include a module that considers current issues and events in tourism. Nevertheless, it is useful to think about what the key contemporary issues are, and their implications for many of the topics that comprise the travel and tourism curriculum. The purpose of this final section, therefore, is to highlight some of these issues. Unlike the preceding sections, no reference is made to exam questions, to 'taking it further', or to key textbooks – a number of current themes and challenges are simply introduced for you to consider within the broader context of studying travel and tourism.

Of course, contemporary issues will, by definition, change over time. Nevertheless, the following are some issues or challenges which are likely to remain predominant in travel and tourism for the foreseeable future.

Crisis and crisis management

As international tourism has grown in scope and scale over the last half-century, so too has the potential for crises and disasters that impact upon tourism. In fact, to the casual observer, it would appear that tourism and tourists have become increasingly subjected to risks, crises and disasters of varying forms and intensity. Certainly, over the last decade or so, international tourism has suffered a number of environmental, political and economic disasters that have not only had a significant impact on tourism both nationally and globally, but which have also occurred with apparently ever-increasing frequency. Most recently, of course, the Asian tsunami had a devastating impact on tourist destinations around the Indian Ocean, but other headline-grabbing events, such as the SARS outbreak, the Bali bombing and the economic crisis in South-east Asia in the late 1990s all impacted upon international tourism.

A number of observations can be made with respect to crises in travel and tourism:

- It is not a new phenomenon: tourism has always been susceptible to external shocks, whether they be economic crises, health scares, environmental disasters, terrorist attacks or wars.
- Disasters may also be 'internal' to the tourism industry; the aviation industry, for example, suffered a spate of crashes in the summer of 2005.
- Crises and disasters are infinitely variable in nature, intensity, duration, impact and recovery time. Some may be short-lived; other crises, such as the political turmoil in Sri Lanka, may have long-term impacts on tourism.
- The effects of crises on the tourism industry tend to be relatively short-term and regionalised. For example, 2001 (the year of 9/11) was only the second year since 1950 that global tourist arrivals actually fell.

Undoubtedly, the spread of tourism around the globe has increased the risk of crises. However, certain questions must be asked. Can some crises be anticipated? Are there ways of preventing crises in tourism? Is it inevitable that crises will continue to occur with greater frequency? And, how can crisis management contribute to minimising the long-term impacts of crises?

Sustainable tourism development

Since the late 1980s, the concept of sustainable development has dominated national and international development policy. Similarly, within the specific context of travel and tourism, the concept of sustainable tourism development has gained worldwide endorsement as the most appropriate approach to tourism development. At the international, national, local and industry level, numerous policy documents, planning guidelines, codes of conduct and statements of good practice and so on have been produced, all promoting or extolling the virtues of sustainable tourism development.

Such widespread acceptance of the concept is not surprising given the growth of environmentalism in general, and the concern over the negative consequences of tourism development in particular. However, questions remain over the viability of the concept – many question both the principles and objectives of sustainable tourism development, particularly as an alternative to mass tourism, and a number of important questions must be addressed. For example, can mass tourism be sustainable? Does the responsibility lie with the tour operators to adopt more responsible practices? Should air transport be subject to an environmental tax? Does ecotourism offer a genuinely sustainable approach to tourism development? Can travel and tourism genuinely contribute to sustainable development, or should it be seen simply as a powerful economic development agent?

Ethics in tourism

Related to the concept of sustainable development, the issue of ethics has become increasingly important in both commercial and social life. Ethics refers to the codes by which human behaviour is guided – how people respond to each other, how they travel, how business is done. In travel and tourism, ethics is concerned with how tourism is managed at the level of both the industry and the individual tourist. Thus, there are two perspectives – human ethics and business ethics, the latter often embraced by what is referred to as corporate social responsibility, or CSR.

While most individuals and organisations would agree that ethical behaviour is a desirable, if not essential objective, particularly within an activity such as travel and tourism, there are a number of problems inherent in implementing an ethical stance, including:

- Ethics are based upon values, not laws; people and businesses can only be encouraged, not enforced, to adopt ethical behaviour. Codes of conduct (for businesses and individuals) are a common means of encouraging ethical behaviour, but their effectiveness is limited.

- Similar to environmental concern, ethical behaviour is seen to be a national not an individual issue. It is difficult to encourage the individual tourist, or tourism business, to act ethically.
- In travel and tourism, the adoption of ethical behaviour on the part of tourists may seem to be contrary to the spirit or meaning of tourism, such as escape, fun, relaxation, and so on.

The World Travel and Tourism Council has endorsed the concept of corporate social responsibility, while the World Tourism Organization has developed a Global Code of Ethics for Tourism. However, given the lack of enforceability of codes of ethics, the profit motive of most tourism businesses, and the reasons why people participate in tourism, how realistic is it to expect both businesses and individuals in tourism to adopt more ethical behaviour? Are there more effective ways than codes of conduct? How can travel and tourism be managed more ethically? Does the only answer lie in greater legislation?

Health issues

Health is frequently a barrier to tourism. That is, concerns about health (or personal safety) may dissuade people to travel to certain destinations where the risk of contracting an illness may be perceived to be high or where an outbreak of a disease results in official advice (i.e. a **travel advisory**) not to travel to a particular destination. For example, an outbreak of plague in India in 1994 resulted in a significant fall in tourism to the subcontinent for a number of weeks, while the impact on tourism of the SARS outbreak in Asia in 2003 was also highly significant.

However, the SARS outbreak was also an example of a particular health-related problem in travel and tourism, namely, the spread of infectious diseases as a result of tourism. In other words, tourists are able to travel to more distant and exotic places or, as a result of greater political freedom, to countries that were once off-limits. While this has opened up opportunities for new travel experiences, it has also placed increasing numbers of tourists at risk of contracting diseases which they then carry home with them – one of the most alarming aspects of the SARS outbreak, for example, was the rapidity with which it travelled across the globe. While the spread of diseases is not yet a major problem it is a challenge that the travel industry and, possibly, governments may have to face up to in the future.

Information technology

Inevitably, information technology is a major contemporary issue in travel and tourism. Where travel technology represented the first revolution in tourism, information technology represents the second. The impact of information technology, particularly the Internet, has been dramatic and far-reaching, fundamentally changing the manner in which travel and tourism is marketed and purchased. At the same time, information technology more generally has made a significant contribution to business practice, underpinning the development of powerful database marketing systems, more efficient resource use and yield management, and so on. In short, access to and use of information through media such as the Internet has revolutionised the business of travel and tourism.

For tourists, the Internet literally presents a window to the world. It has also provided them with greater influence in the chain of distribution, inasmuch as the industry now has to respond to demand rather than creating it – tour operators, travel agencies and principals all face challenges in the way they do business. For tourists, the Internet also represents a challenge in that they now design their own holidays (but also, perhaps, take the responsibility when things go wrong). But how much further can information technology go? Will customers begin to reject the Internet in favour of the 'human touch'? Will virtual travel become a reality?

Changing demands

The demand for tourism has demonstrated consistent growth since the 1950s. Although the annual rate of increase has slowed, international arrivals are expected to continue to grow, reaching an estimated 1.6 billion by 2020 (more than twice the current figure for international arrivals). While only time will tell whether that forecast will prove to be accurate (and there is nothing to suggest that the figures won't be met), some consideration needs to be given to the consequences of such growth. In other words, continuing growth in tourism is seen to be a 'good thing', particularly if the benefits of tourism, such as income and employment, are more widely or equitably enjoyed around the world. However, is it likely that the less developed areas of the world, particularly many of the least developed nations, will benefit from tourism, or will the richer nations or established destinations gain more?

Perhaps more importantly, we need to consider how and where will this growth occur, and what will be the impacts on travel and tourism infrastructure and the environment? Many international airports are already operating at capacity, while air traffic control systems are also stretched at peak periods. As a result, travellers may begin to experience ever-increasing delays, and safety may be compromised. Also, will the increase be within regions or will it be global? For example, will the current economic boom in China result in a significant growth in international travel by the Chinese? And, overall, what will be the environmental consequences of more than doubling the number of international travellers, and providing the facilities and amenities they require?

part three
study, writing and revision skills*

Introduction

If you work your way carefully through this chapter, by the end you should be better equipped to profit from your lectures, benefit from your seminars, construct your essays efficiently, develop effective revision strategies and respond comprehensively to the pressures of exam situations. In the five sections that lie ahead you will be presented with:

- Checklists and bullet points to focus your attention on key issues.
- Exercises to help you to participate actively in the learning experience.
- Illustrations and analogies to enable you to anchor learning principles in everyday events and experiences.
- Worked examples to demonstrate the use of such features as structure, headings and continuity.
- Tips that provide practical advice in a concise form.

In the exercises that are provided, you should decide how much effort you would like to put into each one according to your own individual preferences and requirements. Some of the points in the exercises will be covered in the text either before or after the exercise. Conversely, you might prefer to read each section right through before going back to tackle the exercises. Suggested answers are provided in italics after some of the exercises, so avoid these if you prefer to work through the exercises on your own. The aim is to prompt you to reflect on the material, to remember what you have read and to encourage you to add your own thoughts. Space is provided for you to write your responses down in a

---

*in collaboration with David McIlroy

few words, or you may prefer to reflect on them within your own mind. However, writing will help you to slow down and digest the material and may also enable you to process the information at a deeper level of learning.

Finally, the overall aim of this section is to point you to the keys for academic and personal development. The twin emphases of academic development and personal qualities are stressed throughout. By giving attention to these factors, you will give yourself the toolkit you will need to excel in your studies.

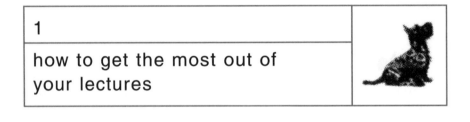

1	
how to get the most out of your lectures	

This section will provide you with tips on how to:

- make the most of your lecture notes
- prepare your mind for new terms
- develop an independent approach to learning
- write efficient summary notes from lectures
- take the initiative in building on your lectures.

Keeping in context

According to higher educational commentators and advisers, the way to achieve the best-quality learning is to set it within an overall learning context. It should be the responsibility of your tutors to provide a context for you to learn in, introducing you, for example, to the broad scope of travel and tourism and the value or importance of studying it either as a subject in its own right or, perhaps, as a future career. However, it is your responsibility to see this overall context, and you can do this even before your first lecture begins. Such a panoramic view can be achieved by becoming familiar with the outline content of both a particular topic and the entire course or study programme. Before you go into each lecture, you should briefly remind yourself of where it fits into the overall scheme of things. Think, for example, of how much more confident you feel when you move into a new city (e.g. to attend university) once you have become familiar with your bearings – where you live in relation to college, shops, stores, buses, trains, places of entertainment, and so on.

The same principle applies to your course – find your way around your study programme and locate the position of each lecture within this overall framework.

Use of lecture notes

It is always beneficial to do some preliminary reading before you enter a lecture. If lecture notes are provided in advance (e.g. electronically), then print these out, read through them and bring them with you to the lecture. You can also insert question marks on issues where you will need further clarification. You will find that some lecturers provide full notes while others prefer to make just outline notes or 'overheads' available – some, of course, might not provide any notes at all! If notes are provided, however, it is important to supplement these with your own notes as you listen – you shouldn't simply rely on notes given to you in advance by your lecturer. In a later section on memory techniques, you will see that humans possess the ability to make 're-learning savings'. In other words, it is easier to learn material the second time round because we have a capacity to hold residual memory deposits. So some basic preparation will equip you with a great advantage – you will be able to 'tune in' and think more clearly about the lecture than you would have done with the preliminary work.

If you set yourself too many tedious tasks at the early stages of your academic programme you may lose some motivation and momentum. A series of short, simple, achievable tasks can give your mind the 'lubrication' you need. For example, you are more likely to maintain preliminary reading for a lecture if you set modest targets, such as reading one or two suggested chapters rather than all of them.

Mastering technical terms

Let us assume that in an early lecture you are introduced to a series of new terms, such as 'paradigm', 'empirical' and 'zeitgeist'. If you are hearing these and other terms for the first time, you could end up with a headache! New words can be threatening, especially if you have to face a string of them in one lecture. The uncertainty about the new terms may impair your ability to benefit fully from the lecture and, therefore, hinder the quality of your learning. Some subjects require technical terms and the use of them is unavoidable (although in travel and tourism, you will find that there are relatively few technical terms). However, when you have heard a term a number of times it will not seem as daunting as it did initially. It is claimed that individuals may have particular strengths in the scope of their vocabulary. Some people may have a good recognition vocabulary – they immediately know what a word means when they read it or hear it in context. Others have a good command of language when they speak – they have an ability to recall words freely. Still others are more fluent in recall when they write – words seem to flow rapidly for them when they engage in the dynamics of writing. You can work at developing all three approaches in your course, and the checklist below the next paragraph may be of some help in mastering and marshalling the terms you hear in lectures.

In terms of learning new words, it will be very useful if you can first try to work out what they mean from their context when you first encounter them. You might be much better at this than you imagine, especially if there is only one word in the sentence that you do not understand. It would also be very useful to buy yourself a small indexed notebook and to use this to build up your own glossary of terms. In this way, you could include a definition of a word, an example of its use, where it fits into a theory and any practical application of it.

Checklist: Mastering terms used in your lectures

- ✓ Read lecture notes before the lectures and list any unfamiliar terms.
- ✓ Read over the listed terms until you are familiar with their sound.
- ✓ Try to work out meanings of terms from their context.
- ✓ Do not suspend learning the meaning of a term indefinitely.
- ✓ Write out a sentence that includes the new word (do this for each word).
- ✓ Meet with other students and test each other on the technical terms.
- ✓ Jot down new words you hear in lectures and check the meaning soon afterwards.

Your confidence will greatly increase when you begin to follow the flow of arguments that contain technical terms, and more especially when you can freely use the terms yourself in speaking and writing.

Developing independent study

The current educational ethos embraces the twin aims of cultivating teamwork/group activities and independent learning. There is not necessarily a conflict between the two; in fact, they should complement each other. For example, if you are committed to independent learning you have more to offer other students when you work in small groups, and you will also be prompted to follow up the leads given by them. Furthermore, the guidelines given to you in lectures are designed to lead you into deeper independent study. The issues raised in lectures are pointers to provide direction and structure for your extended personal pursuit. Your aim should invariably be to build on what you are given, and you should never think of merely returning the bare bones of the lecture material in a coursework essay or exam.

It is always very refreshing to a marker to be given work from a student that contains recent studies that the examiner had not previously encountered.

Note-taking strategy

Note-taking in lectures is an art that you will perfect only with practice and by trial and error. Each student should find the formula that works best for him or her – what works for one, does not necessarily work for another. Some students can write more quickly than others, some are better at shorthand than others, and some are better at deciphering their own scrawl! The challenge will always be to try to find a balance between concentrating on what your lecturer is saying, and making sufficient notes to enable you to comprehend later what you have heard. However, you should try not to let yourself become frustrated by the fact that you will not understand or remember immediately everything you have heard.

> By being present at a lecture, and by making some attempt to understand and think about what you hear, you will already have a substantial advantage over those students who do not attend the lecture.

Guidelines: Note-taking in lectures

- ✓ Develop the note-taking strategy that works best for you.
- ✓ Work at finding a balance between listening and writing.
- ✓ Make some use of optimal shorthand (e.g. a few key words may summarise a story).
- ✓ Too much writing may impair the flow of the lecture for you.
- ✓ Too much writing may impair the quality of your notes.
- ✓ Some limited notes are better than none.
- ✓ Good note-taking may facilitate deeper processing of information.
- ✓ It is essential to 'tidy up' notes as soon as possible after a lecture.
- ✓ Reading over notes soon after lectures will consolidate your learning.

Developing the lecture

Some educationalists have criticised the value of lectures, alleging that they are merely a mode of 'passive learning'. Up to a point, this can certainly be a logical conclusion to arrive at, particularly if students approach lectures in the wrong way, but lecturers can, of course, devise ways of making lectures more interactive. For example, they can make use of interactive handouts or they can ask questions during the lecture, giving 'time out' for students to reflect on these. Other possibilities, depending on the size of the class, are short discussions at given junctures in the lecture or the use of small groups within the session. What is important to remember is the fact that, as a student, you do not have to enter a lecture in passive mode (although you might frequently feel like doing so!). You can ensure that you are not merely a passive recipient of information by taking steps to develop the lecture yourself. This is undoubtedly easier when studying travel and tourism – most people have participated in tourism and, therefore, have their own personal experience on which to draw. Nevertheless, the following list of suggestions will help you take the initiative in developing the lecture content.

Checklist: Ensuring that the lecture is not merely a passive experience

✓ Try to interact with the lecture material by asking questions.

✓ Highlight points that you would like to develop in personal study.

✓ Trace connections between the lecture and other parts of your study programme.

✓ Bring together notes from the lecture and other sources.

✓ Restructure the lecture outline into your own preferred format.

✓ Think of ways in which aspects of the lecture material can be applied.

✓ Design ways in which aspects of the lecture material can be illustrated.

✓ If the lecturer invites questions, make a note of all the questions asked.

✓ Follow up issues of interest that have arisen out of the lecture.

> *You can contribute to this active involvement in a lecture by engaging with the material before, during and after it is delivered.*

2	
how to make the most of your seminars	

The purpose of this section is to help you benefit from seminars, in particular by:

• being aware of the value of seminars
• focusing on links to learning
• recognising qualities you can use repeatedly
• managing potential problems in seminars
• preparing yourself adequately for seminars.

Not to be underestimated

Seminars are often optional in a degree programme and sometimes poorly attended because their value is underestimated. That is, some students may think that the lecture is the only authoritative way to receive quality information. Undoubtedly, lectures play an important role in an academic programme, but seminars have a unique contribution to learning that will complement lectures. Other students may feel that their time would be better spent in personal study. Again, private study is unquestionably essential for personal learning and development but you will, nevertheless, diminish your learning experience if you neglect seminars. If seminars were to be removed from academic programmes, then something really important would be lost.

Seminars have a number of useful features. Attending and contributing to seminars:

- can identify problems that you had not thought of
- can clear up confusing issues
- allows you to ask questions and make comments
- can help you develop friendships and skills for teamwork
- enables you to refresh and consolidate your knowledge
- can help you sharpen motivation and redirect study efforts.

An asset to complement other learning activities

Currently there is an emphasis on variety in higher education – variety in delivery, learning experience, learning styles and assessment methods. The seminar is seen as one element of this variety, playing an important role within the overall scheme of teaching, learning and assessment. In some programmes, the seminars may be directly linked to the assessment task. Whether or not they have such a place in your course, they will provide you with a unique opportunity to learn and develop both your knowledge about travel and tourism and your personal skills of discussion, argument and enquiry.

In a seminar, you will hear a variety of contributions, different perspectives and emphases. You will have both the chance to interrupt and the experience of being interrupted! You will also learn that you can get things wrong and still survive! It is often the case that when one student admits that they did not know some important piece of information, other students quickly follow on to the same admission in the wake of this. If you can learn to ask questions and not feel stupid, then seminars will give you an asset for learning and a lifelong educational quality.

Creating the right climate in seminars

It has been said that we have been given only one mouth to talk, but two ears to listen. One potential problem with seminars is that some students may take a while to learn this lesson. In lectures, your main role is to listen and take notes, but in seminars you need to strike the balance between listening and speaking. It is important to make a start in speaking even if it is just to repeat something that you agree with – the main thing is to have, or try to develop, the confidence to contribute to a discussion. You can also learn to disagree in an agreeable way, without resorting to personal attacks. For example, you might question what someone else has said by asking, 'If that is the case, does that not mean that …'. Conversely, responding to other people's ideas with comments such as, 'that was a really stupid thing to say', or 'I thought you knew better than that', or 'I'm surprised that you don't know that by now' is unlikely to create a friendly climate. Educationalists say that it is important to have the right climate in which to learn, and the avoidance of unnecessary conflict will foster such a climate.

Lecturers use a number of methods to run seminars effectively to ensure that not only are the appropriate issues discussed but also that all students benefit from the experience. If, as often happens, you are asked to lead a seminar, some suggestions are:

- Appoint someone to guide and control the discussion.
- Invite individuals to prepare in advance to make a contribution.
- Hand out agreed discussion questions at some point prior to the seminar.
- Stress at the beginning that no one should monopolise the discussion and emphasise that there must be no personal attacks on any individual (state clearly what this means).
- Encourage quieter students to participate and assure each person that their contribution is valued.

Links in learning and transferable skills

An important principle in learning to progress from shallow to deep learning is developing the capacity to make connecting links between themes or topics and across subjects. This also applies to the various learning activities, such as lectures, seminars, fieldwork, computer searches and private study. Another factor to think about is, 'what skills can I develop, or improve on, from seminars to use across my study programme?' A couple of examples of key skills are the ability to communicate and the capacity to work within a team. These are skills that you will be able to use at various points in your course (transferable), but you are not likely to develop them within the formal setting of a lecture.

EXERCISE

Write out or think about (a) three things that give seminars value, and, (b) three useful skills that you can develop in seminars

(a)

✓ ....

✓ ....

✓ ....

(b)

✓ ....

✓ ....

✓ ....

In the above exercise, for (a) you could have – variety of contributors, flexibility to spend more time on problematic issues and agreed agenda settled at the beginning of the seminar. For (b) you could have – communication, conflict resolution and team work.

> *A key question that you should bring to every seminar – 'How does this seminar connect with my other learning activities and my assessments?'*

An opportunity to contribute

If you have never made a contribution to a seminar before, you may need something to break the ice. It does not matter if your first contribution is only a sentence or two – the important thing is to make a start. One way to do this is to make brief notes as others contribute and, while doing this, a question or two might arise in your mind. If your first contribution is a question, that is a good start. Or it may be that you will be able to point out some connection between what others have said, or identify conflicting opinions that need to be resolved. If you have already begun making contributions, it is important that you keep the momentum going, and do not allow yourself to lapse back into the safe cocoon of shyness. Remember, your opinions or ideas are as valid as anyone else's.

Strategies for benefiting from your seminar experience

In order to benefit from discussions in seminars, the following will point you in the right direction:

✓ Do some preparatory reading.
✓ Familiarise yourself with the main ideas to be addressed.
✓ Make notes during the seminar.
✓ Make some verbal contribution, even a question.
✓ Remind yourself of the skills you can develop.
✓ Trace learning links from the seminar to other subjects/topics on your programme.
✓ Make brief bullet points on what you should follow up.
✓ Read over your notes as soon as possible after the seminar.
✓ Continue discussion with fellow students after the seminar has ended.

If you are required to bring a presentation to your seminar, you might want to consult a full chapter on presentations in a complementary study guide (e.g. McIlroy, 2003). Alternatively, you may be content with the following summary:

✓ Have a practice run with friends.
✓ If using visuals, do not obstruct them.
✓ Check beforehand that all the equipment works.
✓ Space out points clearly on visuals (large and legible).
✓ 'Time-talk' by visuals (e.g. 5 slides × 15-minute talk = 3 minutes per slide).
✓ Make sure your talk synchronises with the slide on view at any given point.
✓ Project your voice so that everyone in the room can hear.
✓ Inflect your voice and do not stand motionless.
✓ Spread eye contact around your audience.

✓ Avoid the twin extremes of fixed gaze at individuals and never looking at anyone.

✓ Better to fall a little short of time allocation than to run over it.

✓ Be selective in what you choose to present.

✓ Map out where you are going and summarise main points at the end.

3	
essay-writing tips	

The purpose of this section is to help you get to grips with the key skills in successful essay writing. Writing effectively is as much an art as a science but, nevertheless, following a number of basic guidelines will help you produce well-structured and academically sound essays. You will find numerous study skills books that deal with the specific challenge of essay writing and they are well worth looking at. This section, however, will help you to:

- engage quickly with the main arguments
- channel your passions constructively
- note your main arguments in an outline
- find and focus on your central topic questions
- weave quotations into your essay.

Getting into the flow

In essay writing, one of your first aims should be to get your mind active and engaged with your subject. Tennis players like to go out onto the court and hit the ball back and forth just before the competitive match begins. This allows them to judge the bounce of the ball, feel its weight against their racket, get used to the height of the net, the parameters of the court and other factors such as temperature, light, sun and the crowd. In the same way, you can 'warm up' for your essay by tossing the ideas to and fro within your head before you begin to write. This will allow you to think within the framework of your topic, and this will be especially important if you are coming to the subject for the first time.

Quite often, ideas will come to you when you are doing something other than sitting at your computer trying to write your essay – for example, you may be out walking or sitting on a bus. You may not even be thinking consciously about your essay when ideas 'hit' you. It is, therefore, useful to keep a notebook with you to write down your thoughts as they come to you – it is surprising how easy it is to forget wonderful ideas!

The tributary principle

A tributary is a stream that runs into a main river as it wends its way to the sea. Similarly, in an essay (or even a longer piece of work, such as a dissertation) you should ensure that every idea you introduce is moving toward the overall theme you are addressing. Your idea might, of course, be relevant to a subheading that is, in turn, relevant to a main heading. However, every idea you introduce is to be a 'feeder' into the flowing theme. In addition to tributaries, there can also be 'distributaries', which are streams that flow away from the river. In an essay, these would represent the ideas that run away from the main stream of thought and leave the reader trying to work out what their relevance might have been. It is one thing to have grasped your subject thoroughly, but quite another to convince your reader that this is the case. Your aim should be to build up ideas sentence by sentence and paragraph by paragraph, until you have communicated your clear purpose to the reader.

In essay writing, it is important not only to include material that is relevant, but also to make linking statements that show the connection to the reader. By including 'signpost' statements, such as 'having explored this issue, it is now logical to consider…', you will both guide the reader through your essay and help clarify your arguments in your own mind.

Listing and linking the key concepts

All subjects will have central concepts that can sometimes be usefully labelled by a single word. Course textbooks may include a glossary of terms and these provide a direct route to the beginning of efficient mastery of the topic. The central words or terms are the essential raw materials that you will need to build upon. Ensure that you learn the words and their definitions, and be able to link the key words together so that in your learning activities you will add understanding to your basic memory work.

> *If possible or logical, it is useful to list your key words under general headings. You may not always see the connections immediately but when you later come back to a problem that seemed intractable, you will often find that your thinking is much clearer.*

EXAMPLE   Write an essay on 'Understanding the motivation for travel and tourism'

You might decide to draft your outline points in the following manner (or you may prefer to use a mind map approach):

Tourist motivation

1 Motivation in the tourism demand process.

- trigger for goal-orientated behaviour

2 Types of motivation.

Extrinsic (social) factors:
Work–tourism relationship

- compensation
- inversion

Family
Reference groups
Society
Consumer culture

Intrinsic (psychological factors):
Psychological needs

- ego-enhancement
- avoidance

An adversarial system

In higher education, students are required to make the transition from descriptive to critical writing. In a sense, a critical approach is similar to a law case where there is both a prosecution and a defence – in other words, you should attempt to consider both sides of an argument. Your concern should be for objectivity, transparency and fairness. No matter how passionately you may feel about a given cause or subject, you must not allow information or arguments to be filtered out because of your personal prejudice. An essay should not become a crusade for a cause in which the contrary arguments are not addressed in an even-handed manner. This means that you should recognise that opposite views are held and that you should at least represent these as accurately as possible.

If you liken the essay-writing process to the hearing of a law case, then your role as the writer is similar to that of a judge; you must ensure that all the evidence is heard, that nothing will compromise either party, and that the outcome (conclusion) is based upon all the evidence presented.

Stirring up passions

The above points do not, of course, mean that you are not entitled to a personal persuasion or to feel passionately about your subject. On the contrary, such feelings may well be a marked advantage if you can bring them under control and channel them into balanced, effective writing (see the example below). Remember, some students may be struggling with the opposite problem – being required to write about a topic that they feel quite indifferent about or have no interest in! As you engage with your topic and toss ideas around in your mind, you will hopefully find that your interest is stimulated, if only at an intellectual level initially. Nevertheless, how strongly you feel about a topic, or how much you are interested in it, may depend on whether you choose the topic yourself or whether it as been given to you as an obligatory assignment. In the latter case, you need to develop the self-discipline to research and write an essay even if you are not particularly interested in the subject – you may, for example, have little interest in the strategic management of hotel chains but being able to consider the challenges facing such hotels is important to your understanding of the accommodation sector of the travel and tourism industry.

It has been said that choosing a dissertation topic is like choosing a spouse, in that you have to live with it for a long time! It is important, therefore, that in a large project, such as a dissertation, that you choose a topic for which you can maintain your motivation, momentum and enthusiasm.

One emotive and subjective issue in travel and tourism is the broad issue of sex tourism. It is, for example, often claimed that tourism causes prostitution in tourism destinations but there are arguments both for and against this position:

EXAMPLE **Arguments for and against tourism as a cause of prostitution**

For

- The relative wealth of tourists allows them to exploit poor women/men in tourism destinations.
- Tourism provides opportunities not available in tourism-generating countries.
- Tourists are unrestricted by social/moral codes of their home society.
- The tourism industry encourages/sells sex-motivated tourism.

Against

- Prostitution may have already existed in the destination prior to the development of tourism.
- Prostitution is 'caused' by the social and economic conditions in the destination society.
- Local authorities could, if they wished, close down the sex industry.
- Local women/men may, in fact, be exploiting tourists.

While there are many other arguments both for and against, this demonstrates the need for a balanced, objective approach.

Structuring an outline

It is a basic principle in all walks of life that structure and order facilitate good communication. Whenever you sense a flow of inspiration to write on a given subject, it is essential that you put this into a structure that will allow your inspiration to be communicated clearly and so that the marker recognises the true quality of your work. For example, you might plan for an introduction, conclusion, three main headings and each of these with several subheadings (see example below). Moreover, you may decide not to include your headings in your final presentation, but just use them initially to structure and balance your arguments (in fact, many examiners prefer not to see subheadings used in formal essays). Once you have drafted this outline, you can then easily sketch an introduction, and you will have been well prepared for the conclusion when you arrive at that point.

> *A good structure will help you to balance the weight of each of your arguments against each other, and arrange your points in the order that will facilitate the fluent progression of your argument.*

EXAMPLE **Write an essay that considers the impact of low-cost airlines on the structure of the international aviation industry**

1 *Introduction.*

- rapid growth in the number of low-cost carriers, particularly in Europe and USA
- background to this growth: liberalisation/deregulation
- examples of low-cost carriers

2 *Characteristics of low-cost operations.*

- low costs
- 'walk-on' seating
- low levels of service
- Internet booking/ticket-less travel
- limited range of aircraft types (service efficiencies)

3 *Limitation of low-cost operations.*

- use of regional airports
- limited distance for efficient operations
- limited levels of service

4 *Conclusions.*

- main impact on short-haul operations
- increase in short-haul air travel at expense of road/rail
- major international airlines must compete on short-haul
- differentiation in short-haul: quality/service vs low-cost
- little impact on longer-haul international operations

Finding major questions

When you are constructing a draft outline for an essay or project, you should ask what is the major question or questions you wish to address. It would be useful to make a list of all the issues that spring to mind that you might wish to tackle. The ability to design a good question is an art form that should be cultivated, and such questions will allow you to impress your assessor with the quality of your thinking.

> *If you construct your ideas around key questions, this will help you to focus your mind and engage effectively with your subject. Your role will be like that of a detective – exploring the evidence and investigating the findings.*

To illustrate the point, consider the example presented below. If you were asked to write an essay about the potential contribution of travel and tourism to the social and economic development of a destination, you might as your starting point pose the following questions.

EXAMPLE   **The role of travel and tourism in development.**
  Initial questions

- What is 'development'?
- What are the characteristics of development?
- How does development occur?
- Why is tourism selected as a means of achieving development?
- How can tourism contribute to development?
- What will limit tourism's developmental contribution?
- Do different forms of tourism result in different degrees or types of development?
- Can tourism contribute to development in both the destination and generating regions?

Rest your case

It should be your aim to give the clear impression that your arguments are not based entirely on hunches, bias, feelings or intuition. In exams and essay questions, it is usually assumed (even if not directly specified) that you will appeal to evidence to support your claims. Therefore, when you write your essay you should ensure that it is liberally sprinkled with citations and evidence. By the time the assessor reaches the end of your work, he or she should be convinced that your conclusions are based on evidence. A fatal flaw to be avoided is to make claims for which you have provided no authoritative source.

Give the clear impression that what you have asserted is derived from recognised and up-to-date sources. It also looks impressive if you spread your citations across your essay rather than compressing them into a paragraph or two at the beginning and end.

Some examples of how you might introduce your evidence and sources are provided below:

According to O'Neil (1999) ...
Wilson (2003) has concluded that ...
Taylor (2004) found that ...
It has been claimed by McKibben (2002) that ...
Appleby (2001) asserted that ...
A review of the evidence by Lawlor (2004) suggests that ...
Findings from an analysis presented by Rea (2003) would indicate that ....

It is sensible to vary the expression used so that you are not monotonous and repetitive, and it also aids variety to introduce researchers' names at various places in the sentence (not always at the beginning). It is advisable to choose the expression that is most appropriate – for example, you can make a stronger statement about reviews that have identified recurrent and predominant trends in findings as opposed to one study that appears to run contrary to all the rest.

Do remember that any evidence included in your essays (tables, graphs, maps and so on) must be fully referenced. You should also be clear in your own mind when you should include page numbers after the date, how to reference electronic/Internet sources and so on. A good way to learn is to see how academics reference their sources in their books or journal articles, although most study guides include a detailed section on referencing.

Careful use of quotations

Although it is desirable to present a good range of cited sources, it is not judicious to present these as 'patchwork quilt' by just simply pasting together what others have said with little thought for interpretative comment or coherent structure. It is a good general point to aim to avoid very lengthy quotes – short ones can be very effective. Aim at blending the quotations as naturally as possible into the flow of your sentences. Also, it is good to vary your practices – sometimes use short, direct, brief quotes (cite the author, year and page number), and at times you can summarise the gist of a quote in your own words. In this case you should cite the author's name and year of publication but leave out the quotation marks and page number.

> Use your quotes and evidence in a manner which demonstrates that you have thought through the issues, and have integrated them in a manner that shows you have been focused and selective in the use of your sources.

In terms of referencing, practice may vary from one discipline to the next, but some general points that will go a long way in contributing to good practice are:

- If a reference is cited in the text, it must be in the list at the end (and vice versa).
- Names and dates in the text should correspond exactly with the list in the references or bibliography.
- The lists of references and bibliography should be in alphabetical order by the surname (not the initials) of the author or first author.
- Any reference you make in the text should be traceable by the reader (they should be able to clearly identify and trace the source).

> Referencing fulfils a number of purposes. Primarily, it demonstrates your knowledge of the literature and your recognition of the contribution of other academics/authors. At the same time, however, it should also enable the reader to find your source for their own interest or knowledge, so your referencing should be as full and accurate as possible.

A clearly defined introduction

In an introduction to an essay, you have the opportunity to define the problem or issue that is being addressed and to set it within context. Resist the temptation to elaborate on any issue at the introductory stage. For example, think of a music composer who throws out hints and suggestions of the motifs that the orchestra will later develop. What he or she does in the introduction is to provide little tasters of what will follow in order to whet the audience's appetite. If you go back to the analogy of the tennis game, you can think of the introduction as marking out the boundaries of the court in which the game is to be played.

If you leave the introduction and definition of your problem until the end of your writing, you will be better placed to map out the directions that will be taken.

EXERCISE

For practice, if you wish, look back at the example (see page 175) on assessing the impacts of low-cost airlines on the international aviation sector. Try to design an introduction for that essay in about three or four sentences.

Conclusion: adding the finishing touches

In the conclusion, you should aim to tie your essay together in a clear and coherent manner. It is your last chance to leave an overall impression in your reader's mind. Therefore, you will at this stage want to do justice to your efforts and not sell yourself short. This is your opportunity to identify where the strongest evidence points or where the balance of probability lies.

A useful trick is to start your conclusion with words to the effect of: 'The purpose of this essay was…', repeating what you wrote in the introduction. This ensures that you have actually done what you set out to do in your essay.

The conclusion to an exam question often has to be written hurriedly under the pressure of time but, with a coursework essay, you have time to reflect on, refine and adjust the content to your satisfaction. It should be your goal to make the conclusion a smooth finish that does justice to the range of content in a summarised, and succinct form. Do not underestimate the value of an effective conclusion. 'Sign off' your essay in a manner that brings closure to the treatment of your subject.

> *The conclusion facilitates the chance to demonstrate where the findings have brought us to date, to highlight the issues that remain unresolved and to point to where future research should take us.*

Top-down and bottom-up clarity

A word processor gives you the opportunity to refine each sentence and paragraph of your essay. Each sentence is like a tributary that leads into the stream of the paragraph that in turn leads into the mainstream of the essay. From a 'top-down' perspective (starting at the top with your major outline points), clarity is facilitated by the structure that you draft in your outline. You can ensure that the subheadings are appropriately placed under the most relevant main heading, and that both sub and main headings are arranged in logical sequence. From a 'bottom-up' perspective (that is, building up the details that 'flesh out' your main points), you should check that each sentence is a 'feeder' for the predominant concept in a given paragraph. When all this is done, you can check that the transition from one point to the next is smooth rather than abrupt.

Checklist: Summary for writing essays

✓ Before you start – have a 'warm up' by tossing the issues around in your head.
✓ List the major concepts and link them in fluent form.
✓ Design a structure (outline) that will facilitate balance, progression, fluency and clarity.
✓ Pose questions and address these in a critical fashion.

✓ Demonstrate that your arguments rest on evidence and spread cited sources across your essay.

✓ Provide an introduction that sets the scene and a conclusion that rounds off the arguments.

In the above checklist, you could also include features such as originality, clarity in sentence and paragraph structure, applied aspects, addressing a subject you feel passionately about and the ability to avoid going off at a tangent.

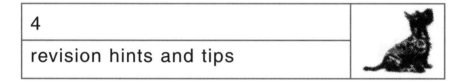

4	
revision hints and tips	

This section will provide you with tips on how to:

- map out your accumulated material for revision
- choose summary tags to guide your revision
- keep well-organised folders for revision
- make use of effective memory techniques
- revise using a combination of bullet points and in-depth reading
- profit from the benefits of revising with others
- attend to the practical exam details that will help keep panic at bay
- use strategies that keep you task-focused during the exam
- select and apply relevant points from your prepared outlines.

The return journey

In the introduction, this Companion was described as a sort of travel guide through the diverse subject of travel and tourism. In the same sense, on a return journey you will usually pass by all the same places that you had already passed when you were outward bound. If you had observed the various landmarks on your outward journey, you would be likely to remember them on your return.

Similarly, revision is a means to 'revisit' what you have encountered before. Familiarity with your material can help reduce anxiety, inspire confidence and fuel motivation for further learning and good performance.

> *If you are to capitalise on your revision period, then you must have your materials arranged and at hand for the time when you are ready to make your 'return journey' through your notes.*

Start at the beginning

Strategy for revision should be on your mind from your first lecture at the beginning of your academic semester. You should be like the squirrel that stores up nuts for the winter. Do not waste any lecture, tutorial, seminar, or group discussion by letting the material evaporate into thin air. Get into the habit of making a few guidelines for revision after each learning activity. Keep a folder, or file, or little notebook that is reserved for revision and write out the major points that you have learned. By establishing this regular practice, you will find that what you have learned becomes consolidated in your mind, and you will also be in a better position to 'import' and 'export' your material both within and across subjects.

> *If you do this regularly, and do not make the task too tedious, you will be amazed at how much useful summary material you have accumulated when revision time comes.*

As part of this process, it is particularly important in travel and tourism to collect a number of case-studies of destinations or organisations in different sectors of the industry both to illustrate your work and to bring it to life. It is surprising how particular examples or cases can be used to illustrate different issues or questions.

Compile summary notes

It would be useful and convenient to have a little notebook or cards on which you can write outline summaries that provide you with an overview of your subject at a glance. You could also use treasury tags to hold different batches of cards together while still allowing for inserts and re-sorting. Such practical resources can be easily slipped into your pocket or bag and produced when you are on the bus or train or while sitting in a traffic jam. They would also be useful if you are standing in a queue or waiting for someone who is not in a rush!

> *There is a part of the mind that will continue to work on problems when you have moved on to focus on other issues. Therefore, if you feed on useful, targeted information, your mind will continue to work on 'automatic pilot' after you have 'switched off'.*

A glance over your notes will consolidate your learning and activate your mind to think further about your subject. Therefore, it would also be useful to make note of the questions that you would like to think about in greater depth. Your primary task is to get into the habit of constructing outline notes that will be useful for revision, and a worked example is provided below.

EXAMPLE   Part of a course on the accommodation sector within the travel industry focuses on organisational growth strategies, particularly franchising.

Your outline revision structure for this might be as follows:

1 Different growth strategies in the international hotel sector.

- organic growth
- acquisition
- joint venture
- franchising
- management contracts
- consortia

2 Benefits of franchising.

For the hotel owner:

- security of an established
  operating system
- internationally recognised brand
- connection to global reservation
  systems
- central/group sales, marketing
  and PR
- availability of training/support
- economies of scale in purchasing
- expert advice: financial,
  property development
- inter-hotel referral of clients

For the franchisor:

- fee income
- strategic growth of organisation/
  wider brand awareness
- no high capital investments
  related to property acquisition

3 Disadvantages of franchising.

For the hotel owner:

- high cost of fees: higher occupancy
  required to compensate
- considerable initial investment
- adaptation difficulties/costs
- dependence on franchisor stability
- loss of individual identity

For the franchisor:

- spread costs of global
  distribution systems across
  large number of properties
- initial setting-up costs
- lack of quality control
  exercised by franchisees

Keep organised records

People who have a fulfilling career have usually developed the twin skills of time and task management. It is worth pausing to remember that you can use your academic training to prepare for your future career in this respect. Therefore, ensure that you do not fall short of your potential because these qualities have not been cultivated. One important tactic is to keep a folder for each subject and divide this topic by topic. You can keep your topics in the same order in which they are presented in your course lectures. Make a numbered list of the contents at the beginning of the folder, and list each topic clearly as it marks a new section in your folder. Another important practice is to place all your notes on a given topic within the appropriate section – don't put off this simple task, do it straight away. Notes may come from a variety of sources, including lectures, seminars, tutorials, Internet searches and personal notes. It is also essential that when you remove these for consultation that you return them to their 'home' immediately after use.

Academic success has as much to do with good organisation and planning as it has to do with ability. The value of the quality material you have accumulated on your academic programme may be diminished because you have not organised it into an easily retrievable form.

EXAMPLE Fun example of an organised record – a history of romantic relationships.

- physical features my girlfriends/boyfriends have shared or differed in
- common and diverse personality characteristics
- shared and contrasting interests
- frequency of dates with each
- places frequented together
- contact with both circles of friends
- use of humour in our communication
- frequency and resolution of conflicts
- futual generosity
- courtesy and consideration
- punctuality
- dress and appearance

Let's imagine that you have had five girlfriends/boyfriends over the last few years. Each of the five names could be included under all of the above subjects. You could then compare them with each other – looking at what they had in common and how they differed. Moreover, you could think of the ones you liked best and least, and then look through your dossier to establish why this might have been. You could also judge who had most and least in common with you and whether or not you are more attracted to those who differed most from you. The questions open to you can go on and on. The real point here is that you will have gathered a wide variety of material that is organised in such a way that it will allow you to use a range of evidence to come up with some satisfactory and authoritative conclusions – if that is possible in matters so directly related to the heart!

Use past papers

Revision will be very limited if it is confined to memory work. You should by all means read over your revision cards or notebook and keep the picture of the major facts in front of your mind's eye. It is also, however, essential that you become familiar with previous exam papers so that you will have some idea of how the questions are likely to be framed. Therefore, build up a good range of past exam papers (especially recent ones) and add these to your folder.

If you think over previous exam questions, this will help you not only to recall what you have deposited in your memory, but also to develop your understanding of the issues. The questions from past exam papers, and further questions that you have developed yourself, will allow you to think about what questions may be asked and, more importantly, how you would answer them.

EXAMPLE **Evaluate the pleasures and problems of keeping a pet**

Immediately you can see that you will require two lists and you can begin to work on documenting your reasons under each as below:

Problems	*Pleasures*
• vet and food bills	• companionship
• restrictions on holidays/ weekends away	• fun and relaxation
• friends may not visit	• satisfaction from caring
• allergies	• cuddles
• smells and cleanliness	• contact with other pet owners
• worries about leaving pet alone	• good distraction from problems

You will have also noticed that the word 'evaluate' is in the question – so your mind must go to work on making judgements. You may decide to work through problems first and then through pleasures, or it may be your preference to compare point by point as you go along. Whatever conclusion you come to may be down to personal, subjective preference but at least you will have worked through all the issues from both stand-points. The lesson is to ensure that part of your revision should include critical thinking as well as memory work.

> *You cannot think adequately without the raw materials provided by your memory deposits.*

Employ effective mnemonics (memory aids)

The Greek word from which 'mnemonics' is derived refers to a tomb – a structure that is built in memory of a loved one, friend or respected person. 'Mnemonics' can be simply defined as aids to memory – devices that will help you recall information that might otherwise be difficult to retrieve from memory. For example, if you find an old toy in the attic of your house, it may suddenly trigger a flood of childhood memories associated with it. Mnemonics can, therefore, be thought of as keys that open memory's storehouse.

> 1   *If you can arrange your subject matter in a logical sequence this will ensure that your series of facts will also connect with each other and one will trigger the other in recall.*
> 2   *You can use memory devices either at the stage of initial learning or when you later return to consolidate.*

Visualisation is one technique that can be used to aid memory. For example, the location method is where a familiar journey is visualised and you can 'place' the facts that you wish to remember at various landmarks along the journey, such as a bus stop, a car park, a shop, a store, a bend, a police station, or a traffic light. This has the advantage of making an association of the information you have to learn with other material that is already firmly embedded and structured in your memory. Therefore, once the relevant memory is activated, a dynamic 'domino effect' will be triggered. However, there is no reason why you cannot use a whole toolkit of mnemonics. Some examples and illustrations of these are presented below.

Visualisation

Turn information into pictures. The example given about the problems and pleasures of pets could be envisaged as two tug-of-war teams that pull against each other. You could visualise each player as an argument and have the label written on his or her T-shirt. The war could start with two players and then be joined by another two and so on. In addition, you could compare each player's weight to the strength of each argument. You might also want to make use of colour – your favourite colour for the winning team and the colour you dislike most for the losers!

Alliteration's artful aid

Find a series of words that all begin with the same letter. See page 189 on the experiments of Ebbinghaus.

Peg system

'Hang' information on to a term so that when you hear the term you will remember the ideas connected with it (i.e. an umbrella term). In the earlier example of tourist motivation, 'extrinsic' and 'intrinsic' factors are two such terms (see page 172).

Hierarchical system

This is a development of the previous point with higher order, middle order and lower order terms. For example, you could think of the continents of the world (higher order), and then, below, group the countries belonging to them (middle order), followed by countries' cities, rivers and mountains (lower order).

Acronyms

Take the first letter of all the key words and make a word form these. An example used in strategic or marketing management is, of course, SWOT – Strengths, Weaknesses, Opportunities and Threats.

Mind maps

These have become very popular. They allow you to develop ideas using lines that stretch out from the central idea and then to develop the subsidiary ideas in the same way. It is a little like the pegging and hierarchical methods combined and turned sideways! The method has the advantage of giving you the complete picture at a glance, although they can become a complex work of art!

Rhymes and chimes

These are words that rhyme and end with a similar sound, such as commemoration, celebration, or anticipation. They provide another dimension to memory work by including sound. Memory can be enhanced when information is processed in various modalities, for example, hearing, seeing, speaking and visualising.

A confidence booster

At the end of the 19th century, Ebbinghaus and his assistant memorised lists of nonsense words (words that could not be remembered by being attached to meaning), and then endeavoured to recall these. They discovered that:

- Some words could be recalled freely from memory while others appeared to be forgotten.
- Words that could not be recalled were later recognised as belonging to the lists (i.e. were not new additions).
- When the lists were jumbled into a different sequence, the experimenters were able to re-jumble them into the original sequence.
- When the words that were 'forgotten' were learned again, the learning process was much easier the second time (i.e. there was evidence of re-learning savings).

The four points of this experiment can be remembered by alliteration: Recall, Recognition, Reconstruction and Re-learning savings. This experiment has been described as a confidence booster because it demonstrates that memory is more powerful than is often imagined, especially when we consider that Ebbinghaus and his assistant did not have the advantage of processing the meaning of the words.

Alternate between methods

It is not sufficient, of course, to present outline points in response to an exam question (although it is better to do this than nothing if you have run out of time in your exam). Your aim should be to put 'meat on the bones' by adding substance, evidence and arguments to your basic points. You should work at finding the balance between the two methods – outline revision cards might be best reserved for short bus journeys, whereas extended reading might be better employed for longer revision slots at home or in the library. Your ultimate goal should be to bring together an effective working approach that will enable you to face your exam questions comprehensively and confidently.

> When revising, it is useful to alternate between scanning over your outline points and reading through your notes, articles, chapters and so on in an in-depth manner. Also, the use of different times, places and methods will provide you with the variety that might prevent monotony and facilitate freshness.

EXAMPLE Imagine that you are doing a course on the human body

Your major outline topics might be:

- names, positions and purpose of bones in the body
- names and positions of organs in the body
- the organs and chemicals associated with digestion
- composition, function and routes of blood
- parts and processes of the body associated with breathing
- components and dynamics of the nervous and lymphatic systems
- structure, nature and purpose of the skin
- role of the brain in controlling and mediating the above systems

This outline would be your overall, bird's-eye view of the course. You could then choose one of the topics and have all your key terms under that. For example, under digestion you might have listed: mouth, oesophagus, stomach, duodenum, intestine, liver, vagus nerve, hypothalamus, hydrochloric acid and carbohydrates. In order to move from memory to understanding you would need to consider the journey of food through the human digestive system.

If you alternate between memory work and reading, you will soon be able to think through the processes by just looking at your outlines.

Revising with others

If you can find a few other students to revise with, this will provide another fresh approach to the last stages of your learning. First, ensure that others carry their workload and are not merely using the hard work of others as a short cut to success. Of course, you should think of group sessions as one of the strings on your violin, but not the only string. This collective approach would allow you to assess your strengths and weaknesses (showing you where you are off-track), and to benefit from the resources and insights of others. Before you meet, you can each design some questions for the whole group to address. The group could also go through past exam papers and discuss the points that might provide an effective response to each question. It should not be the aim of the group to provide standard and identical answers for each group member to mimic. Group work is currently deemed to be advantageous by educationalists and teamwork is a desirable employability quality.

Each individual should aim to use their own style and content while drawing on and benefiting from the group's resources.

EXERCISE

Make a list of the advantages and disadvantages of revising in small groups.

Advantages	Disadvantages
1	1 ....
2	2 ....
3	3 ....
4	4 ....
5	5 ....

Can the disadvantages be eliminated or at least minimised?

___

Checklist: Good study habits for revision time

✓ Set a date for the 'official' beginning of revision and prepare for 'revision mode'.

✓ Do not force cramming by leaving revision too late.

✓ Take breaks from revision to avoid saturation.

✓ Indulge in relaxing activities to give your mind a break from pressure.

✓ Minimise or eliminate use of alcohol during the revision season.

✓ Get into a good rhythm of sleep to allow renewal of your mind.

✓ Avoid excessive caffeine, especially at night so that sleep is not disrupted.

✓ Try to adhere to regular eating patterns.

✓ Try to have a brisk walk in fresh air each day, e.g. in the park.

✓ Avoid excessive dependence on junk food and snacks.

___

EXERCISE

Write your own checklist on what you would add to the revision process to ensure it was not just a memory exercise.

✓ _____

✓ _____

✓ _____

✓ _____

✓ _____

___

In the above exercise, what you could add to memory work during revision might include using past exam papers, setting problem-solving tasks, doing drawings to show connections and directions between various concepts, explaining concepts to peers in joint revision sessions, devising your own mock exam questions.

5	
exam tips	

This section is designed to help you succeed in your exams. It will provide you with tips on how to:

- develop strategies for controlling your nervous energy
- tackle worked examples of time and task management in exams
- attend to the practical details associated with the exam
- stay focused on the exam questions
- link revision outlines to strategy for addressing exam questions.

Handling your nerves

Exam nerves are not unusual and it has been concluded that test anxiety arises because of the perception that your performance is being evaluated, that the consequences are likely to be serious and that you are working under the pressure of a time restriction. However, it has also been asserted that the activation of the autonomic nervous system is adaptive in that it is designed to prompt us to take action in order to avoid danger. If you focus on the task at hand rather than on feeding a downward negative spiral in your thinking patterns, this will help you keep your nerves under control. In the run-up to your exams your can practise some simple relaxation techniques that will help you bring stress under control.

> *It is a very good thing if you can interpret your nervous reactions positively, but the symptoms are more likely to be problematic if you interpret them negatively, pay too much attention to them, or allow them to interfere with your exam preparation or performance.*

Practices to reduce or buffer the effects of exam stress

- listening to music
- going for a brisk walk

- simple breathing exercises
- some muscle relaxation
- watching a movie
- enjoying some laughter
- doing some exercise
- relaxing in a bath (with music if preferred)

The best choice is going to be the one (or combination) that works best for you – perhaps to be discovered by trial and error. Some of the above techniques can be practised on the morning of the exam, and even the memory of them can be used just before the exam. For example, you could run over a relaxing tune in your head, and have this echo inside your head as you enter the exam room. The idea behind all this is that, first, stress levels must come down and that, second, relaxing thoughts will serve to displace stressful reactions. It has been said that stress is the body's call to take action, but anxiety is a maladaptive response to that call.

It is important you are convinced that your stress levels can come under control, and that you can have a say in this. Do not give anxiety a vacuum to work in.

Time management, with examples

The all-important matter as you approach an exam is to develop the belief that you can take control over the situation. As you work through the list of issues that you need to address, you will be able to tick them off one by one. One of the issues you will need to be clear about before the exam is the length of time you should allocate to each question. Sometimes this can be quite simple (although, it is always necessary to read the instructions carefully) – for example, if two questions are to be answered in a two-hour paper, you should allow one hour for each question. If it is a two-hour paper with one essay question and five shorter answers, you could allow one hour for the essay and twelve minutes each for the shorter questions. However, you always need to check the weighting for the marks on each question, and you will also need to deduct whatever time it takes you to read over the paper and to choose your questions. More importantly, give yourself some practice on the papers you are likely to face.

Remember to check if the structure of your exam paper is the same as on previous years, and do not forget that excessive time on your 'strongest' question may not compensate for very poor answers to other questions. Also, ensure that you read the guidelines carefully in the exam.

See if you can work out a time management strategy in each of the following scenarios.

EXERCISE

Examples for working out the division of exam labour by time.

1. A three-hour paper with four compulsory questions (equally weighted in marks).

2. A three-hour paper with two essays and ten short questions (each of the three sections carry one-third of the marks).

3. A two-hour paper with two essays and 100 multiple-choice questions (half the marks are on the two essays, and half on the multiple-choice section).

Make sure you know the structure of the exam. Get into the calculating frame of mind and be sure to have the calculations done before the exam. Also, deduct the time taken to read over the paper in allocating time to each question.

Suggested answers to previous exercise

1 This allows 45 minutes for each question (4 questions × 45 minutes = 2 hours). However, if your allow 40 minutes for each question this will give you 20 minutes (4 questions × 5 minutes) to read over the paper and plan your outlines.

2 In this example, you can spend 1 hour on each of the two major questions, and 1 hour on the ten short questions.

For the two major questions you could allow 10 minutes for reading and planning on each, and 50 minutes for writing. In the ten short questions, you could allow 6 minutes in total for each (10 questions × 6 minutes = 60 minutes). However, if you allow approximately 1 minute reading and planning time, this will allow 5 minutes for writing each answer.

3 *In this case, you have to divide 120 minutes by three questions – this allows 40 minutes for each. You could, for example, allow 5 minutes for reading/planning each essay and 35 minutes for writing (or 10 minutes for reading/planning and 30 minutes for writing). After you have completed the two major questions you are left with 40 minutes to tackle the 100 multiple-choice questions.*

You may not be able to achieve total precision in planning time for tasks, but you will have a greater feeling of control and confidence if you have some reference points to guide you.

Task management, with examples

After you have decided on the questions you wish to address, you then need to plan your answers. Some students prefer to plan all outlines and draft work at the beginning, while others prefer to plan and address one answer before proceeding to address the next question. Decide on your strategy before you enter the exam room and stick to your plan. When you have done your draft outline as rough work, you should allocate an appropriate time for each section. This will prevent you from excessive treatment of some aspects while falling short on others. Such careful planning will help you achieve balance, fluency and symmetry.

Be aware of time limitations and this will help you to write succinctly; stay focused on the task and this will prevent you from dressing up your responses with unnecessary padding.

Some students put as much effort into their rough work as they do into their exam essay. An over-elaborate mind map may give the impression that the essay is little more than a repetition of this detailed structure, and that the quality of the content has suffered because too much time was spent on the plan.

EXERCISE

Try the following exercise.

Work within the time allocated for the following outline, allowing for one hour on the question. Deduct ten minutes taken at the beginning for choice and planning.

Discuss whether it is justifiable to ban cigarette smoking in pubs and restaurants.

1 Arguments for a ban

    (a) Health risks by sustained exposure to passive smoking.

    (b) Employees (such as students) suffer unfairly.

    (c) Children accompanying parents may also be victims.

2 Arguments against a ban

    (a) Risks may be exaggerated.

    (b) Dangerous chemicals and pollutants in the environment ignored by governments.

    (c) Non-smokers can choose whether to frequent smoking venues.

3 Qualifying suggestions

    (a) Better use of ventilation and extractor fans.

    (b) Designated non-smoking areas.

    (c) Pubs and restaurants should be addressed separately in relation to a ban.

Attend to practical details

This short section is designed to remind you of the practical details that should be attended to in preparation for an exam. There are always students who turn up late, or to the wrong venue or for the wrong exam, or not at all! Check and re-check that you have all the details of each exam correctly noted. What you don't need is to arrive late and then have to tame your panic reactions. The exam season is the time when you should aim to be at your best.

> *Turn up to the right venue in good time so that you can quieten your mind and bring your stress under control.*

Make note of the following details and check that you have taken control of each one.

Checklist: Practical exam details

- ✓ Check that you have the correct venue.
- ✓ Make sure you know how to locate the venue before the exam day.
- ✓ Ensure that the exam time you have noted is accurate.
- ✓ Allow sufficient time for your journey and consider the possibility of delays.
- ✓ Bring an adequate supply of stationery and include back-up.
- ✓ Bring a watch for your time and task management.
- ✓ You may need some liquid such as a small bottle of still water.
- ✓ You may also need to bring some tissues.
- ✓ Observe whatever exam regulations your university/college has set in place.
- ✓ Fill in the required personal details before the exam begins.

Control wandering thoughts

In a simple study conducted in the 1960s, Ganzer found that students who frequently lifted their heads and looked away from their scripts during exams tended to perform poorly. This makes sense because it implies that the students were taking too much time out when they should have been on task. One way to fail your exam is to get up and walk out of the test room, but another way is to 'leave' the test room mentally by being preoccupied with distracting thoughts. These distracting thoughts may be either related to the exam itself or totally irrelevant to it. However, the net effect of both these forms of intrusion is to distract you from the task at hand and debilitate your test performance. Read over the two lists of distracting thoughts presented below.

Typical test-relevant thoughts (evaluative)	Characteristic test-irrelevant thoughts (non-evaluative)
• I wish I was better prepared. • What will the examiner think? • Others are doing better than me. • What I am writing is nonsense. • Can't remember important details.	• Looking forward to this weekend. • Which video should I watch tonight? • His/her remark really annoyed me yesterday. • Wonder how the game will go on Saturday. • I wonder if he/she really likes me?

Research has consistently shown that distracting, intrusive thoughts during an exam are more detrimental to performance than stressful symptoms such as sweaty palms, dry mouth, tension, trembling and so on. Moreover, it does not matter whether the distracting thoughts are negative evaluations related to the exam or are totally irrelevant to the exam. The latter may be a form of escape from the stressful situation.

Practical suggestions for controlling wandering thoughts

- Be aware that this problem is detrimental to performance.
- Do not look around to find distractions.
- If distracted, write down 'keep focused on task'.
- If distracted again, look back at above and continue to do this.
- Start to draft rough work as soon as you can.
- If you struggle with initial focus then re-read or elaborate on your rough work.
- If you have commenced your essay, re-read you last paragraph (or two).
- Do not throw fuel on your distracting thoughts – starve them by re-engaging with the task at hand.

Links to revision

If you have followed the guidelines given for revision, you will be well equipped with outline plans when you enter the exam room. You may have chosen to use headings and subheadings, mind maps, hierarchical approaches or just a series of simple mnemonics. Whatever method you choose to use, you should be furnished with a series of memory triggers that will open the treasure-house door for you once you begin to write.

> Although you may have clear templates with a definite structure or framework for organising your material, you will need to be flexible about how this should be applied to your exam questions.

For example, imagine that films are one of the topics on which you will be examined. You decide to memorise lists of films that you are familiar with under categorical headings in the following manner:

Romantic comedy	War/History/Fantasy	Space/Invasion
Notting Hill	Braveheart	Star Wars
Pretty Woman	Gladiator	Independence Day
Along came Polly	First Knight	Alien
Four Weddings and a Funeral	Troy	Men in Black

Adventure/Fantasy	Horror/Supernatural
Harry Potter	Poltergeist
Lord of the Rings	The Omen
Alice in Wonderland	Sixth Sense
Labyrinth	What Lies Beneath

The basic mental template might be these and a few other categories. You know that you will not need every last detail, although you may need to select a few from each category. For example, you might be asked to:

1 Compare and contrast features of the comedy and horror genres.

2 Comment on films that have realistic moral lessons in them.

3 Discuss films that might be construed as an exercise in propaganda.

4 Identify films where the characters are more important than the plot and vice versa.

Some questions will put a restriction on the range of categories you can use (1), while others will allow you to dip into any category (2, 3 and 4). A question about fantasy would allow you scope across various categories.

> Restrict your material to what is relevant to the question, but bear in mind that this may allow you some scope.

Art of 'name-dropping'

In most topics at university, including travel and tourism, you will be required to cite studies as evidence for your arguments and to link these to the names of researchers, scholars or theorists. It will help if you can use the correct dates or at least the correct decades, and it is good to demonstrate that you have used contemporary sources and have done some independent work. A marker will have dozens, if not hundreds, of scripts to work through and they will know if you are just repeating the same phrases from the same sources as everyone else. There is inevitably a certain amount of this that must go on, but there is room for you to add fresh and original touches that demonstrate independence and imagination.

> Give the clear impression that you have done more than the bare minimum and that you have enthusiasm for the subject. Also, spread the use of researchers' names across your exam essay rather than compressing them into, for example, the first and last paragraphs.

Flight, fight or freeze

As previously noted, the autonomic nervous system (ANS) is activated when danger or apparent danger is imminent. Of course, the threat does not have to be physical, as in the case of an exam, a job interview, a driving test or a TV appearance. Indeed, the ANS can be activated even at the anticipation of a future threat. However, the reaction is more likely to be stronger as you enter into the crucial time of testing or challenge. Symptoms may include deep breathing, trembling, headaches, nausea, tension, dry mouth and palpitations. How should we react to these once they have been triggered? A postman might decide to run away from a barking dog and run the risk of being chased and bitten. A second possible response is to freeze on the spot – this might arrest the animal in its tracks, but is no use in an exam situation. In contrast, to fight might not be the best strategy against the dog, but will be more productive in an exam. That is, you are going into the exam room to 'tackle' the questions, and not to run away from the challenge before you.

The final illustration below uses the analogy of archery to demonstrate how you might take control in an exam.

Lessons from archery

- Enter the exam room with a quiver full of arrows – all the points you will need to use.
- Eye up the target board you are to shoot at – choose the exam questions.
- Stand in a good position for balance and vision – prepare your time management.
- Prepare your bow and arrow and take aim at the target – keep focused on the task at hand and do not be sidetracked.
- Pull the string of the bow back to get maximum thrust on the arrow – match your points to the appropriate question.
- Aim to hit the board where the best marks are (bull's-eye or close) – do not be content with the minimum standard such as a mere pass.
- Pull out arrows and shoot one after another to gain maximum hits and advantage – do not be content with preparing one or two strong points.
- Make sure your arrows are sharp and the supporting bow and string are firm – choose relevant points and support them with evidence.
- Avoid wasted effort by loose and careless shots – do not dress up your essay with unnecessary padding.

EXERCISE

Write your own checklist on the range of combined skills and personal qualities that you will need to be at your best in an exam.

- ✓ ....
- ✓ ....
- ✓ ....
- ✓ ....
- ✓ ....

With reference to the above exercise, skills might include: critical thinking, time and task management, focus on issues and quick identification of problems to address. Personal qualities might include factors such as confidence, endurance, resilience and stress control.

6

tips on interpreting essay and exam questions

Interpreting exam questions is not always easy. This section provides you with tips on how to:

- focus on the issues that are relevant and central
- read questions carefully and take account of all the words
- produce a balanced critique in your outline structures
- screen for the key words that will shape your response
- focus on different shades of meaning between 'critique', 'evaluate', 'discuss' and 'compare and contrast'.

What do you see?

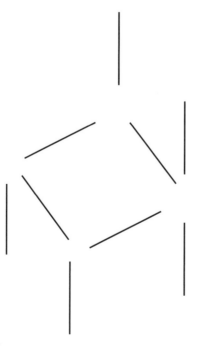

Figure 3.1   Visual illusion

The suggested explanation for visual illusions is the inappropriate use of cues; that is, we try to interpret three-dimensional figures in the real world with the limitations of a two-dimensional screen (the retina in the eye). We use cues such as shade, texture, size, or background to interpret distance, motion, shape and so on, and we sometimes use these inappropriately. Another visual practice we engage in is to 'fill in the blanks' or join up the lines (as in the case of the nine lines above – we might assume to be a chair). Our tendency is to impose the nearest similar and familiar template on that which we think we see. The same occurs in the social world – when we are introduced to someone of a different race we may (wrongly) assume certain things about them. The same can also apply to the way you read exam or essay questions. In these cases, you are required to 'fill in the blanks' but what you fill in may be the wrong interpretation of the question. This is especially likely if you have primed yourself to expect certain questions to appear in an exam, but it can also happen in coursework essays. Although examiners do not deliberately design questions to trick you or trip you up, they cannot always prevent you from seeing things that were not designed to be there. When one student was asked what the four seasons are, the response given was, 'salt, pepper, mustard and vinegar'. This was not quite what the examiner had in mind!

Go into the exam room, or address the coursework essay well prepared, but be flexible enough to structure your learned material around the slant of the question.

A politician's answer

Politicians are renowned for refusing to answer questions directly or for evading them through raising other questions. A humorous example is that when a politician was asked, 'Is it true that you always answer questions by asking another?', the reply given was, 'Who told you that?' Therefore, make sure that you answer the set question, although there may be other questions that arise out of this for further study that you might want to highlight in your conclusion. As a first principle, you must answer the set question and not another question that you had hoped for in the exam or essay.

Do not leave the examiner feeling like the person who interviews a politician and goes away with the impression that the important issues have been side-stepped.

EXAMPLE   Discuss the strategies for improving the sale of fresh fruit and vegetables in the marketplace at the point of delivery to the customer

Directly relevant points

- stall and fruit kept clean
- well presented/arranged produce
- use of colour and variety
- position of stall in market (e.g. smells)
- use of free samples
- appearance and manner of assistants
- competitive prices

Less relevant points

- advantages of organic growth
- arguments for vegetarianism
- cheaper transport for produce
- value of locally grown produce
- strategies for pest control in growth
- arguments for refrigeration in transit
- cheaper rents for markets

Although some of the points listed in the second column may be relevant to sales overall, they are not as directly relevant to sales 'in the marketplace at the point of delivery to the customer'. If the question had included the quality of the produce, then some of those issues should be addressed. Also, it could be argued that some of these issues could be highlighted on a board at the stall – for example, 'Only organically grown produce is sold at this stall'. So, some of the points could be mentioned briefly in this way without going off at a tangent.

> Be ready to resist the wealth of fascinating material at your disposal that is not directly relevant to your question.

Missing your question

A student bitterly complained after an exam that the topic he had revised so thoroughly had not been tested in the exam. The first response to that is that students should always cover enough topics to avoid selling themselves short in the exam – the habit of 'question spotting' is always a risky game to play. However, the reality in the anecdotal example was that the question the student was looking for was there, but he had not seen it. He had expected the question to be couched in certain words and he could not find these when he scanned over the questions in blind panic. Therefore, the simple lesson is always read over the questions carefully, slowly and thoughtfully. This practice is time well spent.

> *You can miss the question if you restrict yourself to looking for a set form of words and if you do not read over all the words carefully.*

Write it down

If you write down the question you have chosen to address, and perhaps quietly articulate it with your lips, you are more likely to process fully its true meaning and intent. Think of how easy it is to misunderstand a question that has been put to you verbally because you have misinterpreted the tone or emphasis.

> *If you read over the question several times, you should be aware of all the key words and will begin to sense the connections between the ideas, and you will envisage the possible directions you should take in your response.*

Take the following humorous example:

1 What is that on the road ahead?

2 What is that on the road, a head?

Question (1) calls for the identification of an object (what is that?), but question (2) has converted this into an object that suggests there has been a decapitation! Ensure that you understand the direction the question is pointing you towards. One word in the question that is not properly attended to can throw you completely off-track as in the following example:

1 Discuss whether the love of money is the root of all evil.

2 Discuss whether money is the root of all evil.

These are two completely different questions as (1) suggests that the real problem with money is inherent in faulty human use – that is, money itself may not be a bad thing if it is used as a servant and not a master, whereas (2) may suggest that behind every evil act that has ever been committed money is likely to have been implicated somewhere in the motive.

Pursue a critical approach

In degree courses, you are usually expected to write critically rather than merely descriptively, although it may be necessary to use some minimal descriptive substance as the raw material for your debate.

EXAMPLE   Evaluate the evidence of whether the American astronauts really walked on the moon or whether this was a stage-managed hoax in a studio

Arguments for studio hoax

- Why is the flag blowing on the moon?
- Explain the shadows.
- Why are there no stars?
- Why is there little dust blowing on landing?
- Can humans survive passing through the radiation belt?

Arguments for really walking on the moon

- Communicates with laser reflectors left on the moon.
- Retrieved rocks show patterns that are not earthly.
- How could such a hoax be protected?
- American activities were monitored by the Soviets.
- Plausible explanations for arguments against walking.

Given that the question is about a critical evaluation of the evidence, you would need to address the issues one by one from both standpoints. What you should not do is digress into writing about the physical characteristics of the Beagle spaceship or the astronauts' suits. Neither should you be drawn into a lengthy description of lunar features and contours even if you have in-depth knowledge of these.

Analyse the parts

In an effective sports team, the end product is always greater than the sum of the parts. Similarly, a good essay cannot be constructed without reference to the parts. Furthermore, the parts will arise as you break down the question into the components it suggests to you. Although the breaking down of a question into components is not sufficient for an excellent essay, it is a necessary starting point.

> *To achieve a good response to an exam or essay question, aim to integrate all the individual issues presented in a manner that gives shape and direction to your efforts.*

EXAMPLE 1: Discuss whether the preservation and restoration of listed buildings is justified.

Two parts to this question are clearly suggested – preservation and restoration, and you would need to do justice to each in your answer. Other issues that arise in relation to these are left for you to suggest and discuss. Examples might be finance, prioritisation, poverty, beauty, culture, modernisation, heritage and tourism.

EXAMPLE 2: Evaluate the advantages and disadvantages of giving students course credit for participation in experiments.

This is a straightforward question in that you have two major sections – advantages and disadvantages. You are left with the choice of the issues that you wish to address and you can arrange these in the order you prefer. Your aim should be to ensure that you do not have a lopsided view of this even if you feel quite strongly one way or the other.

EXAMPLE 3: Trace in a critical manner Western society's changing attitudes to the corporal punishment of children.

In this case, you might want to consider the role of governments, the church, schools, parents and the media. However, you will need to have some reference points to the past as you are asked to address the issue of change. There would also be scope to look at where the strongest influences for change arise and where the strongest resistance comes from. You might argue that the changes have been dramatic or evolutionary.

Give yourself plenty of practice at thinking of questions in this kind of way – both with topics on and not on your course. Topics not on your course that really interest you may be a helpful way to 'break you in' to this critical way of thinking.

Luchins and learning sets

In a series of experiments, Luchins allowed children to learn how to solve a problem that involved pouring water from and into a series of jugs of various sizes and shapes. He then gave them other problems that could be solved by following the same sequence. However, when he later gave them another problem that could be solved through a simpler sequence, they went about solving it through the previously learned procedure. In this case, the original approach was more difficult but it had become so set in the children's minds that they were blinded to the shorter, more direct route.

EXAMPLE   How much did the wealthy Scottish man leave behind?

The story is told of a wealthy Scottish man who died and no one in his village knew how much he had left behind. The issue was debated and gossiped about for some time, but one man claimed that he knew how much the man had left. He teased all the debaters and gossips in the village night after night. Eventually he let his big secret out and the answer was that the rich man had left 'all of it' behind! No one in the village had been able to work out the mischievous man's little ruse because of the convergent thinking style they used. Some exam questions may require you to be divergent in the way you think (that is, there is not just one obvious solution to the problem). This may mean being like a detective in the way you investigate and solve the problem. The only difference is that you may need to set up the problem as well as the solution!

Get into the habit of 'stepping sideways' and looking at questions from several angles. The best way to do this is by practice on, for example, previous exam papers.

Checklist: Ensuring that questions are understood before being fully addressed

✓ Read over the chosen question several times.
✓ Write it down to ensure that it is clear.
✓ Check that you have not omitted any important aspect or point of emphasis.
✓ Ensure that you do not wrongly impose preconceived expectations on the question.
✓ Break the question into parts (dismantle and rebuild).

EXERCISE

Write your own checklist on any additional points of guidance for exams that you have picked up from tutors or textbooks.

✓ ....
✓ ....
✓ ....
✓ ....
✓ ....

When asked to discuss

Students often ask how much of their own opinion they should include in an essay. In a discussion, when you raise one issue, another one can arise out of it. One tutor used to introduce his lectures by saying that he was going to 'unpack' the arguments. When you unpack an object (such as a new desk that has to be assembled), you first remove the overall packaging, such as a large box, and then proceed to remove the covers from all the component parts. After that, you attempt to assemble all the parts, according to the given design, so that they hold together in the intended manner. In a discussion, your aim should be not just to identify and define all the parts that contribute, but also to show where they fit (or don't fit) into the overall picture.

Although the word 'discuss' implies some allowance for your opinion, remember that this should be informed opinion rather than groundless speculation. Also, there must be direction, order, structure and end project.

Checklist: Features of a response to a 'discuss' question

✓ Contains a chain of issues that lead into each other in sequence.

✓ Clear shape and direction is unfolded in the progression of the argument.

✓ Underpinned by reference to findings and certainties.

✓ Identification of issues where doubt remains.

✓ Tone of argument may be tentative but should not be vague.

If a critique is requested

One example that might help clarify what is involved in a critique is the hotly debated topic of the physical punishment of children. It would be important in the interest of balance and fairness to present all sides and shades of the argument. You would then look at whether there is available evidence to support each argument, and you might introduce issues that have been coloured by prejudice, tradition, religion and legislation. It would be an aim to identify emotional arguments, arguments based on intuition and to get down to those arguments that really have solid evidence-based support. Finally, you would want to flag up where the strongest evidence appears to lie and you should also identify issues that appear to be inconclusive. It would be expected that you should, if possible, arrive at some certainties.

EXERCISE

Write your own checklist for the features of a critique. You can either summarise the above points, or use your own points or a mixture of the two.

✓ ....

✓ ....

✓ ....

✓ ....

✓ ....

If asked to compare and contrast

When asked to compare and contrast, you should be thinking in terms of similarities and differences. You should ask what the two issues share in common, and what features of each are distinct. Your preferred strategy for tackling this might be to first work through all the similarities and then through all the contrasts (or vice versa). Conversely, you might work through a similarity and contrast followed by another similarity and contrast and so on.

EXAMPLE   **Compare and contrast the uses of tea and coffee as beverages**

Similarities

- usually drunk hot
- can be drunk without food
- can be taken with a snack or meal
- can be drunk with milk
- can be taken with honey, sugar or sweeteners
- both contain caffeine
- both can be addictive

Contrasts

- differences in taste
- tea perhaps preferred at night
- differences in caffeine content
- coffee more bitter
- coffee sometimes taken with cream or whisky
- each perhaps preferred with different foods
- coffee preferred for hangover

When you compare and contrast you should aim to paint a true picture of the 'full landscape'.

Whenever evaluation is requested

EXAMPLE   **TV soap opera director**

Imagine that you are a TV director for a popular soap opera. You have observed in recent months that you have lost some viewers to an alternative soap opera on a rival channel. All is not yet lost because you still have a loyal hard core of viewers who have remained faithful.

Your programme has been broadcast for ten years and there has, until recently, been little change in viewing figures. The rival programme has used some fresh ideas and new actors and has a big novelty appeal. It will take time to see if their level of viewing can be sustained, but you run the risk that you might lose some more viewers at least in the short term. Conversely, with some imagination you might be able to attract some viewers back. However, there have been some recent murmurings about aspects of the programme being stale, repetitive and predictable. You have been given the task of evaluating the programme to see if you can ascertain why you have retained the faithful but lost other viewers, and what you could do to improve the programme without compromising the aspects that work. In your task you might want to, review past features (retrospective), outline present features (perspective) and envisage positive future changes (prospective).

This illustration may provoke you to think about how you might approach a question that asks you to evaluate some theory or concept in your own academic field of study. Some summary points to guide you are presented below:

- Has the theory/concept stood the test of time?
- Is there a supportive evidence base that would not be easily overturned?
- Are there questionable elements that have been or should be challenged?
- Does more recent evidence point to a need for modification?
- Is the theory/concept robust and likely to be around for the foreseeable future?
- Could it be strengthened through being merged with other theories/concepts.

EXERCISE

Write your own checklist on what you remember or understand about each of the following: 'discuss', 'compare and contrast', 'evaluate' and 'critique' (just a key word or two for each). If you find this difficult, then you should read the section again and then try the exercise.

✓ ....

✓ ....

✓ ....

✓ ....

It should be noted that the words presented in the above examples might not always be the exact words that will appear on your exam script; for example, you might find 'analyse', or 'outline' or 'investigate'. The best advice is to check over your past exam papers and familiarise yourself with the words that are most recurrent.

In summary, this section has been designed to give you reference points to measure where you are at in your studies and to help you map out the way ahead in manageable increments. It should now be clear that learning should not merely be a mechanical exercise, such as just memorising and reproducing study material. Quality learning also involves making connections between ideas, thinking at a deeper level by attempting to understand your material, and developing a critical approach to learning. However, this cannot be achieved without the discipline of preparation for lectures, seminars and exams, or without learning to structure your material (headings and subheadings), and to set each unit of learning within its overall context in your subject and programme. An important device in learning is to develop the ability to ask questions (whether written, spoken or silent). Another useful device in learning is to illustrate your material and use examples that will help make your study fun, memorable and vivid. It is useful to set problems for yourself that will allow you to think them through and find solutions, and therefore, enhance the quality of your learning.

On the one hand, there are the necessary disciplined procedures such as preparation before each learning activity and consolidation afterwards. It is also vital to keep your subject materials in organised folders so that you can add/extract/replace materials when necessary. On the other hand, there is the need to develop personality qualities such as feeding your confidence, fuelling your motivation and turning stress responses to your advantage. This section has presented strategies to guide you through finding the balance between these organised and dynamic aspects of academic life.

Your aim should be to become an 'all-round student' who engages in and benefits from all the learning activities available to you (lectures, seminars, tutorials, computing, labs, discussions, library work, and so on), and to develop all the academic and personal skills that will put you in the driving seat to academic achievement. It will be motivating and build your confidence if you can recognise the value of these qualities, both across your academic programme and beyond graduation to the world of work. They will also serve you well in your continued commitment to lifelong learning.

glossary	

Acculturation

When two cultures come into contact, one gradually takes on the characteristics of the other.

Adventure tourism

Tourism that involves exciting, new or adventurous experiences or activities.

Alienation

A sense of placelessness, of not belonging, of meaninglessness in modern society.

All-inclusive

A holiday where all services, facilities and entertainment are included in the price.

Allocentric

Allocentric refers to tourists who are outgoing, adventurous, risk-takers.

Alternative tourism

A term that collectively describes forms of tourism that are an alternative to mass tourism.

Anomie

See **alienation**.

Architectural pollution

Visual pollution created by the building of inappropriate structures, such as large, multi-storey hotels, that do not fit with local styles and scale.

Augmented product

The additional or 'value-added' benefits of a product or service beyond the **'core' product**.

Authenticity   Usually meaning genuine or real, in tourism it refers to places or events that are 'traditional' (i.e. pre-modern/undeveloped) or certain types of travel experiences.

Backward linkages   Where the development of tourism stimulates other sectors of the destination economy, such as farming/food production.

Barriers to travel and tourism   Factors, such as wars, terrorism, health scares and so on, that act to limit the growth of tourism.

Business travel   Travel undertaken for the purpose of conducting business.

Cabotage   The right of an airline based in one country to operate between two other countries.

Chain hotel   A hotel that is part of a larger group, either through direct ownership or an alliance arrangement, such as franchising or management contracts.

Chain of distribution   The chain along which a product passes, from the producer to the consumer.

Classification   The classifying of accommodation providers by the facilities provided (e.g. number of en-suite bathrooms), but not by the quality.

Clusters   Groups of businesses related by product or markets that work together for mutual benefit.

Commodification   Cultural objects or events not normally available for sale are commodified when they are purchased by tourists; they become a tourism commodity consumed by tourists for a price.

Consumer culture   The practice of consumption (buying or having things) has a cultural significance as well as fulfilling utilitarian needs. Usually, it is associated with creating self-identity or status.

Core product	The basic or main product, such as a seat on a plane or a room in a hotel.
Critical mass	The volume or number of attractions necessary to ensure a constant and appropriate flow of tourists to a destination.
CTO	Caribbean Tourism Organization, which promotes tourism to the Caribbean, and collects and disseminates research data.
Cultural impacts	The long-term impacts on a destination society's culture or way of life.
Dark tourism	Tourism to sites or attractions that are associated with death and disaster.
Day tripper	A tourist on a day visit from home.
Demand curve	Graph that depicts the relationship between the price and demand for a good or service. Typically, as the price rises, demand falls and vice versa.
Democratisation of tourism	The process whereby travel and tourism has been transformed from an exclusive activity into one increasingly available to the masses.
Deregulation	The process within the USA of removing restrictive trade practices and increasing competition within the airline sector.
Directional selling	Travel retailers favouring or promoting their parent company's products.
Disintermediation	The removal or leap-frogging of intermediaries (wholesalers/retailers) in the **chain of distribution** between producers and customers.
Domestic tourism	Tourists travelling/taking holidays in their own country.

Dynamic packaging   The process whereby customers create their own package holiday from flights, accommodation and services sold on the same website.

Economic impacts   The economic costs and benefits to the destination of developing tourism.

Ecotourism   A contentious term that describes tourism in natural areas, which is mutually beneficial to the environment, local communities and tourists themselves.

Edutainment   A form of experience where education is combined with entertainment.

Ego-enhancement   A motivational factor characterised by the need to feel better about oneself; to achieve personal reward from the tourism experience.

Elasticity of demand/supply   The responsiveness of demand or supply to changes in price.

Environmental impacts   The positive and negative consequences of tourism on the destination's physical environment.

E.tailing   Retailing utilising information technology, specifically the Internet.

E.tourism   A term that collectively refers to the use of information and communication technologies in tourism.

Excursionist   A tourist on a brief trip not involving an overnight stay. Typically, the term refers to on-shore trips by cruise ship passengers.

Five freedoms   The freedoms necessary for international airlines to operate on specified routes.

Flagship attraction   The major attraction at a destination, which supports the development of other, smaller attractions and associated facilities for tourists.

Fordist production	A method of mass production 'invented' by Henry Ford, characterised by high set-up costs, low unit costs, standardized products and production, and the production line.
GDS	Global distribution system, a worldwide computer-based reservation system.
Grading	The qualitative assessment of the facilities and services provided by an accommodation establishment (e.g. its star rating).
Grand Tour	A circuit of Europe undertaken by the wealthy during the 17th and 19th centuries.
Heritage attractions	Attractions that represent or are related to a destination's social, cultural or natural history.
Horizontal integration	Integration within the same sector of the tourism industry (at the same level in the **chain of distribution**).
Hospitality industry	The industry that embraces hotels (lodging) and catering (the provision of food, drink and, where relevant, entertainment).
Hotel consortium	A group of independent hotels that work together for economies of scale in marketing and purchasing.
Hub-and-spoke systems	International airlines fly out of major (hub) airports; they also fly shorter, usually domestic routes (spokes) into the hub as feeders for international flights.
Inclusive tour	Also called a package tour, where two or more elements of a holiday are included in the total price.
Independent hotel	A hotel that is not part of a chain but that may belong to a consortium.
Inseparability	A characteristic of a service, whereby the production and consumption of a service cannot be separated.

Intermediaries	'Middle-men' in the tourism **chain of distribution**, between producers (hotels, airlines, etc.) and consumers (tourists). Tour operators and travel agents are intermediaries.
International development	The process of socio-economic development at the global level.
International tourism	Tourism that involves travel across national borders.
International tourism receipts	The spending of international tourists measured at the destinational, regional, national or international level.
International tourist arrivals	The number of international tourists visiting a destination or country.
Inversion	For tourists, the temporary reversal of their normal life.
Island tourism	Tourism that occurs to and on islands.
ITC	Inclusive tour by charter flight.
ITX	Inclusive tour by scheduled flight.
Least developed countries	The forty or so poorest countries in the world.
Liberalisation	The process within Europe of removing restrictive trade practices and increasing competition within the airline sector.
Liminality	Where tourists have passed through the threshold of their normal lives to an existence where normal rules or routines are temporarily suspended.
Load factors	The proportion of an aircraft's seats that must be sold to break even. Charter flights or low-cost airlines have much higher load factors than scheduled flights.

Long haul	Flights that are over four hours in duration.
Ludic	Forms of tourist behaviour that can be described as play, usually unrestricted by conventional social rules of the tourist's home society.
Macro-economics	The study of the total effects of economic phenomena affecting the local, national or international economy.
Marine tourism	A form of special-interest tourism related to an interest in the sea and marine life.
Market segmentation	The practice of dividing markets into subgroups.
Market segments	Subgroups of total markets that share similar characteristics.
Marketing mix	Often referred to as the four 'Ps', the marketing mix represents the variables that businesses manipulate to achieve their marketing objective.
Mass tourism	The movement of large numbers of tourists to holiday destinations, most commonly associated with summer-sun package tourism.
Micro-economics	Economic analysis at the level of the individual people or businesses.
Multiples	Large travel agency chains (as distinct from independent travel retailers) often owned by a tour operator.
Multiplier effect	The extent to which the value of direct tourist expenditure is multiplied by successive indirect and induced expenditure in the destination.
National tourist board	Usually a public sector organisation that has the responsibility for marketing and developing a county's tourism sector.

New tourist
Contrasted with the mass package tourist, the new tourist is more adventurous, environmentally aware, flexible, quality conscious and so on.

Occupancy level
The measure of the number/proportion of a hotel's rooms or beds that are sold either at a point in time or averaged over a period.

Opportunity costs
A term in economics referring to the potential cost of rejecting one course of action in favour of another.

Package tour
A holiday that is a combination of two or more elements, typically transport and accommodation.

PATA
The Pacific Asia Tourism Association, which promotes tourism in the Pacific Asia region as well as providing information, undertaking research and supporting education and training in tourism.

Periodicity
A term to describe different levels of demand over a period, such as a week.

Physical carrying capacity
The capacity of a destination, attraction or facility to absorb tourists.

Place marketing
The process of identifying a place as a 'place product' and promoting it to meet visitors' needs.

Pleasure periphery
The tourist receiving countries that are increasingly distant from the main ('core') tourism-generating countries.

Post-tourist
Postmodern tourists, who seek variety and who view tourism as a game.

Primary data
Original information generated by research.

Principals
Producers within the travel industry, including airlines, hotels and attractions.

Pro-poor tourism   Tourism development that purposefully contributes to the socio-economic improvement of the word's poorer societies.

Psychocentric   The opposite of **allocentric**, psychocentrics are inwardly focused, unadventurous and risk-averse.

Pull factors   Characteristics of a destination that pull tourists towards choosing it for a holiday.

Push factors   Personal, psychological factors or needs that push or motivate tourists to participate in tourism.

Reference group   A social group against which an individual measures himself/herself, or judges his/her own values and behaviour.

Regression   The return to a child-like existence, to nature or to innocence.

Religious tourism   A form of tourism that is undertaken wholly or partly for religious reasons.

Room rates   The prices charged for a hotel room. These are often lower than the 'rack rate' (the published price for a room).

Rural tourism   Tourism that occurs in rural areas/the countryside, and is traditionally considered to be rural in character.

Seasonality   Recurring, and usually regular, fluctuations in the demand for tourism to a particular destination.

Secondary data   Information that already exists in the public domain.

Service industry   A business that 'produces' services as opposed to physical goods.

Short haul   Flights that are up to four hours in duration.

Short take-off and landing (STOL)	Aircraft that are able to use short runways, usually at airports close to urban centres.
SMEs	Small- to medium-sized enterprises.
Social impacts	The immediate positive and negative consequences of tourism development on destination societies.
Societal marketing	An approach to marketing that reflects an organisation's social and environmental responsibility.
Special interest tourism	Tourism that is motivated by a specific activity, interest or hobby.
Sport tourism	Tourism involving participation in or attendance at sporting events.
Staged authenticity	Rituals, events, shows and other performances that appear authentic but are artificially constructed or staged out of context for the benefit of tourists.
Strategic alliance	Where two or more businesses, such as airlines, collaborate to gain competitive advantage.
Strategic drift	The loss of focus or direction experienced by organisations that do not have a strategy.
Supply curve	A graph that depicts the relationship between the cost and supply of a product or service.
Sustainable tourism development	Tourism that, ideally, contributes positively to the sustainable socio-economic development of the destination.
Symbiosis	A mutually beneficial relationship between, for example, tourism and the destination environment.
Total tourism product	The complete tourism experience from leaving home to returning.

Tourism demand process	The process through which tourists select, experience and evaluate tourism.
Tourism development models	Different conceptual models of how tourism may be developed.
Tourism industry	The organisations and businesses that collectively provide or facilitate tourism experiences.
Tourism satellite account	A measure of the total economic contribution of tourism (direct and indirect) to a country's economy.
Tourism system	The concept of tourism as an interlinking system involving three regions: the generating, transit and destination regions.
Tourist motivation	The process by which an individual's needs are translated into goal-oriented behaviour; the trigger that starts the tourism demand process.
Tourist typologies	Categorisations of tourists based upon different parameters.
Travel advisory	Official government advice on the safety of travel to destinations.
Travel career ladder	As tourists become more experienced, they 'climb the ladder' of tourism, seeking different, more adventurous or individual experiences.
Urban–rural continuum	A term that refers to the increasing 'rurality' of the countryside the more distant it lies from the urban fringe.
Urban tourism	Tourism that occurs in towns and cities.
VALS	Values and Lifestyle Scale, a market segmentation model based on people's needs, wants and attitudes.

Vertical integration Integration between organisations higher up (backwards) or further down (forwards) the **chain of distribution**.

Visitor management The process of managing the behaviour of tourists to minimise their negative impact on the destination environment.

Wine tourism A type of special interest tourism that is motivated by an interest in wine.

World Tourism Organization The world's leading tourism organisation, entrusted by the United Nations with the development and promotion of tourism.

World Travel and Tourism Council An organisation whose members are chief executives of major travel and tourism businesses and which works to promote the economic benefits of tourism development.

Yield management Maximising revenue from the sale of hotel rooms, flights or holidays by raising or lowering the price according to demand.

Youth tourism All forms of tourism undertaken by young people, typically the 15–24 age group.

references

Ansoff, I. (1987) *Corporate Strategy*. London: Penguin.

Boniface, B. and Cooper, C. (2001) *Worldwide Destinations: The Geography of Travel and Tourism*. Oxford: Butterworth-Heinemann.

Bramwell, B. and Lane, B. (eds) (1994) *Rural Tourism and Sustainable Rural Development*. Clevedon: Channel View Publications.

Bull, A. (1995) *The Economics of Travel and Tourism*, 2nd edition, Harlow: Longman.

Burns, P. and Holden, A. (1995) *Tourism: A New Perspective*. Hemel Hempstead: Prentice Hall.

Burton, R. (1995) *Travel Geography*, 2nd edition. London: Pitman.

Butler, R. (1980) 'The concept of a tourism area cycle of evolution', *Canadian Geographer*, 24: 5–12.

Butler, R., Hall, C.M. and Jenkins, J. (eds) (1998) *Tourism and Recreation in Rural Areas*. Chichester: John Wiley & Sons.

Cohen, E. (1972) 'Towards a Sociology of International Tourism', *Social Research*, 39 (1): 64–82.

Cooper, C., Fletcher, J., Fyall, A., Gilbert, D. and Wanhill, S. (2005) *Tourism: Principles and Practice*. Harlow: Pearson Education.

Dann, G. (1981) Tourist motivation: an appraisal. *Annals of Tourism Research*, 8 (2), 187–219.

Doganis, R. (2004) *The Airline Business in the 21st Century*. London: Routledge.

Ebbinghaus, H. (1885/1913) *Memory: A Contribution to Experimental Psychology*. New York: Columbia University Press.

Evans, N., Campbell, D. and Stonehouse, G. (2003) *Strategic Management for Travel and Tourism*. Oxford: Butterworth-Heinemann.

Fyall, A., Garrod, B. and Leask, A. (eds) (2003) *Managing Visitor Attractions: New Directions*. Oxford: Butterworth-Heinemann.

Ganzer, V.J. (1968) 'Effects of audience presence and test anxiety on learning and retention in a serial learning situation', *Journal of Personality and Social Psychology*, 8: 194–99.

Gunn, C. (1994) *Tourism Planning: Basics, Concepts, Cases*. London: Taylor and Francis.

Hall, C.M. (2000) *Tourism Planning: Policies, Processes and Relationships.* Harlow: Pearson Education.

Holden, A. (2000) *Environment and Tourism.* London: Routledge.

Holloway, J.C. (2002) *The Business of Tourism,* 6th edition. Harlow: Pearson Education.

Holloway, J.C. (2004) *Marketing for Tourism,* 4th edition. Harlow: Financial Times Pearson Education.

Horner, S. and Swarbrooke, J. (1996) *Marketing Tourism, Hospitality, and Leisure in Europe.* London: International Thomson Business Press.

Inskeep, E. (1991) *Tourism Planning: An Integrated and Sustainable Development Approach.* New York: Van Nostrand Reinhold.

Jafari, J. (1989) 'Sociocultural dimensions of tourism: an English language literature review', in J. Bystrzanowski (ed.), *Tourism as a Factor of Change: A Sociocultural Study.* Vienna: Vienna Centre, pp. 17–60.

Johnson, G. and Scholes, J. (2002) *Exploring Corporate Strategy,* 7th edition. Harlow: Pearson Education.

Kotler, P., Bowen, J. and Makens, J. (2002) *Marketing for Hospitality and Tourism,* 3rd edition. Upper Saddle River, NJ: Pearson Education.

Krippendorf, J. (1987) *The Holiday Makers.* Oxford: Heinemann.

Law, C. (2002) *Urban Tourism: The Visitor Economy and the Growth of Large Cities.* London: Continuum.

Laws, E. (1997) *Managing Packaged Tours.* London: International Thomson Business Press.

Luchins, A.S. (1942) 'Mechanisms in problem solving: the effects of *Einstellung*', *Psychological Monographs*, 54 (248).

Lumsden, L. and Page, S. (eds) (2004) *Tourism and Transport: Issues and Agenda for the New Millennium.* Oxford: Elsevier.

MacCannell, D. (1999) *The Tourist: A New Theory of The Leisure Class.* Berkeley, CA: University of California Press.

Maslow, A. (1943) A theory of human motivation', *Psychological Review*, 50, 370–96.

Mathieson, A. and Wall, G. (1982) *Tourism: Economic, Physical and Social Impacts.* New York: Longman.

McIlroy, D. (2003) *Studying at University: How to be a Successful Student.* Sage: London.

McKercher, R. (1993) 'Some fundamental truths about tourism: understanding tourism's social and environmental impacts', *Journal of Sustainable Tourism*, 1 (1): 1–16.

Middleton, V. (1994) *Marketing in Travel and Tourism,* 2nd edition. Oxford: Butterworth-Heinemann.

Mill, R. and Morrison, A. (1998) *The Tourism System: An Introductory Text.* Dubuque, Iowa: Kendall/Hunt Publishing.

Opperman, M. and Chon, K. (1997) *Tourism in Developing Countries.* London: International Thomson Business Press.

Page, S. (1995) *Urban Tourism*. London: International Thomson Business Press.

Page, S. (1999) *Transport and Tourism*. Harlow: Longman.

Page, S. (2003) *Tourism Management: Managing for Change*. Oxford: Butterworth-Heinemann.

Page, S. and Getz, D. (1997) *The Business of Rural Tourism*. London: International Thomson Business Press.

Page, S. and Hall, C.M. (2003) *Managing Urban Tourism*. Harlow: Pearson Education.

Pearce, D. (1989) *Tourist Development,* 2nd edition. New York: Longman.

Pender, L. (2001) *Travel Trade and Transport: An Introduction*. London: Continuum.

Pender, L. and Sharpley, R. (2005) *The Management of Tourism*. London: Sage Publications.

Plog, S. (1977) 'Why destination areas rise and fall in popularity', in E. Kelly (ed.), *Domestic and International Tourism*. Wellesley, MA: Institute of Certified Travel Agents.

Porter, M. (1980) *Competitive Strategy: Techniques for Analysing Industries and Competitors*. New York: Free Press.

Roberts, L. and Hall, D. (2001) *Rural Tourism and Recreation: Principles to Practice*. Wallingford: CABI.

Ryan, C. (2003) *Recreational Tourism: Demands and Impacts*. Clevedon: Channel View Publications.

Seaton, A. and Bennett, M. (1996) *Marketing Tourism Products: Concepts, Issues, Cases*. London: Thomson International Business Press.

Shackley, M. (2001) *Managing Sacred Sites*. London: Continum.

Sharpley, R. (ed.) (2002) *The Tourism Business: An Introduction*. Sunderland: Business Education Publishers.

Sharpley, R. (2003) *Tourism, Tourists and Society,* 3rd edition. Huntingdon: Elm Publications.

Sharpley, R. and Sharpley, J. (1997) *Rural Tourism: An Introduction*. London: Thomson International Business Press.

Sharpley, R. and Telfer, D. (2002) *Tourism and Development: Concepts and Issues*. Clevedon: Channel View Publications.

Shaw, G. and Williams, A. (2002) *Critical Issues in Tourism: A Geographical Perspective,* 2nd edition. Oxford: Blackwell Publishers.

Smith, V. (1977) *Hosts and Guests: The Anthropology of Tourism*. Philadelphia: University of Pennsylvania Press.

Swarbrooke, J. (2000) *The Development and Management of Visitor Attractions, 2nd Edition*. Oxford: Butterworth-Heinemann.

Swarbrooke, J. and Horner, S. (1999) *Consumer Behaviour in Tourism*. Oxford: Butterworth-Heinemann.

Tribe, J. (1997) *Corporate Strategy for Tourism*. London: International Thomson Business Press.

Tribe, J. (2004) *The Economics of Recreation, Leisure and Tourism*. Oxford: Butterworth-Heinemann.

index